Shattering the Glasshouse

Breaking A Cycle of Dysfunctional Behaviours

Paul A. Blake M.A.

Copyright

ISBN 978-976-97120-6-5

Cover design by Words Worthit Publishers

Published by Words Worthit Publishers

Available on Amazon Kindle and online stores

Contents

Preface

For much of my early life, I lived behind the walls of what I now call *the family glasshouse*, a fragile world where pain was carefully hidden, appearances were everything, and honesty came at a price. From the outside, our family looked whole, but on the inside, cracks were spreading fast. I didn't understand it then, but those invisible fractures were shaping how I saw myself, how I loved, and how I related to others.

Looking back, I realize that what I called "normal" was actually dysfunction passed from one generation to the next. Arguments, silence, and pride became our family traditions. We learned to pretend that everything was fine, even when our souls were aching. It wasn't until I began my own journey with God that I saw how deeply this brokenness had affected me and how desperately I needed to be healed.

This book was born out of that realization. *Shattering the Glasshouse* is not about blaming anyone. It's about facing the truth that healing will never come through silence or denial. It's about courage, the courage to look at where we've come from and decide that the story will not end there. My hope is that by sharing my own journey, marked by failure, forgiveness, and faith, you will see that it is possible to rise from the debris of dysfunction and build something new.

Shattering the glasshouse is not an act of rebellion; it's an act of redemption. It means exposing the pain we've hidden, naming the things we were taught not to talk about, and allowing God to shine His light through our cracks. Healing doesn't happen overnight, and it doesn't erase the past, but it gives us a chance to live differently, to love better, forgive freely, and create a legacy of wholeness instead of hurt.

This is my story. It's also an invitation for you to look at your own glasshouse and decide that it's time to let the light in.

Introduction

Every one of us carries the weight of where we come from. For years, I carried mine quietly, pain wrapped in pride, fear disguised as strength. Growing up in a family where love and hurt often lived in the same room, I learned early how to survive without truly healing. I thought that if I worked hard enough, achieved enough, or laughed loudly enough, I could silence the echoes of the past. But pain doesn't stay buried; it finds its way to the surface, often when we least expect it.

When I became a Christian, I began to see my story differently. God didn't erase my past; He revealed it. He showed me that every broken piece of my life could become part of something beautiful if I would allow Him to use it. My dysfunction wasn't the end of my story it was the beginning of my transformation.

Shattering the Glasshouse is a story about that transformation. It's about how awareness brings healing, how forgiveness opens doors, and how faith restores what pain has stolen. This is not a book of blame, but of awakening. It's about breaking free from the cycles that hold families hostage: cycles of silence, shame, and denial, and learning how to live with honesty, grace, and courage.

In these pages, I share the lessons I've learned from both my family's struggles and my own failures. You'll see moments of pain, but you'll also find hope. You'll see how faith guided me from brokenness to restoration, and how I discovered that God's purpose often shines brightest through our cracks.

If you've ever felt trapped by your past or burdened by your family's history, I want you to know that healing is possible. This book is my testimony that no matter how shattered life feels, God can rebuild it piece by piece. Together, we can learn to live beyond dysfunction and discover what it truly means to be whole.

In the chapters ahead, I invite you to journey with me through the stages of healing, from recognizing dysfunction, to confronting pain, to forgiving, accepting, and rebuilding through faith. Each chapter is part reflection, part revelation, and part roadmap for transformation. My prayer is that as you turn each page, you will begin to see your own glasshouse differently, and find the courage to let God's light in.

Chapter One

Breaking the Cycle: Understanding the Myth of Generational Curses

The Questions That Follow Us

Having observed my extended family over the years, I've often asked myself a painful, but necessary question, "Why do certain dysfunctional behaviours keep recurring across generations? Why do we seem to end up stuck in the conflicts, repeating the same patterns?"

In the Caribbean, one of the most common explanations is to blame these recurring struggles on "generational curses." But I do not believe in generational curses, not in the mystical sense many people describe.

What I believe is this: Dysfunctional behaviours, if left unchecked, become stumbling blocks for future generations. They are not chains placed on us by unseen forces; They are inherited beliefs, habits, wounds, and responses that resurface over time unless someone chooses to interrupt them.

How Dysfunction Gets Mistaken for Destiny

Growing up in a rural Jamaica, I realized how easily we accept dysfunction when we dress it up as a generational curse. We convince ourselves that destructive traits, toxic behaviours, and difficult personalities are simply "in the blood." And once we believe that we resign ourselves to the idea that nothing can change.

This mindset is deeply woven into Caribbean culture. In moments of conflict, I often heard phrases like:

- "Bad luck a falla wi."
- "A jus suh mi family dem stay."
- "Crasses a falla wi."
- "It inna dem blood."
- "Dem have bad blood."

These sayings may sound harmless on the surface, but they shape identity.

They determine how families see themselves, respond to problems, and make decisions, often with long-term negative consequences.

When Dysfunction Becomes the Family Language

As a child, these phrases were part of daily life. I heard them from aunts, uncles, grandparents, cousins, and even neighbours. Without realizing it, those words shaped my thinking well into my teenage years.

Children don't just learn by instructions, they absorb culture. They mirror the actions, beliefs, and language of the people around them. And without intervention, those patterns become the blueprint for adult life.

When we copy the behaviours around us, we unknowingly reinforce the same dysfunction in our own lives. Even today, many of us are still fighting to break free from cycles we did not choose.

Awareness: The First Step Toward Freedom

No generation is *destined* to repeat the behaviours of the one before it. Change is possible, if there is the courage to challenge what we have **normalized**. I am living **proof** of this truth.

My siblings and I made a conscious decision to do things differently, and that choice became the spark that ignited transformation. But transformation doesn't begin with change; it begins with awareness.

You cannot change what you refuse to acknowledge. What many call a generational curse is often simply the unwillingness of family members to believe that life can be different.

When dysfunction is accepted as unchangeable, the cycle continues unchecked. Hurt, pain, resentment, unforgiveness, and anger become a way of life. Families become breeding grounds for conflict, emotional wounds, and even violence. It is much easier to blame a curse than to confront the root of the issue.

The Cultural Myth of Generational Curses

We must not buy the lie that things cannot change. They can. The old saying, "Where there is a will, there is a way," has guided my own journey out of years of dysfunction. We are still a work in progress, but each year brings growth, healing, and renewed hope.

Breaking the Cycle

Breaking a generational pattern doesn't happen overnight, it's a process that begins with awareness. When I recognized how much of my own behaviour came from what I saw growing up, it changed everything. I started questioning my habits, my words, and my reactions. Was I repeating what I resented? Or was I rewriting my story?

Below are some of the lessons that helped me start that journey:

1. **Exercise Patience:** Healing takes time. Families built on dysfunction won't transform in a day, and neither will you. Be patient with yourself and others as you learn to do things differently.

2. **Forgive, Even When It Hurts:** Forgiveness isn't weakness, it's the release that allows healing to begin. You don't forgive because the person deserves it; you forgive because you deserve peace.

3. **Seek Knowledge and Support**: Education changes everything. Whether it's counselling, books, or spiritual guidance, learn what healthy relationships look like. You can't fix what you don't understand.

4. **Build New Habits:** Decide what kind of family culture you want to pass on. Be intentional about showing love, setting boundaries, and communicating openly.

5. **Invite God into the Process:** Healing without God is like trying to mend glass with your bare hands, you'll only end up bleeding. His wisdom and grace make transformation possible.

Breaking the cycle begins with honesty, with God, with yourself, and with your family. When we stop calling dysfunction "destiny," we begin to walk in freedom. Generational curses lose their power when truth and grace take their place.

Generational Curses: Another Perspective

A Hard but Necessary Truth

"Generational curses are really lazy declarations of pathologies and patterns of learned and inherited traumas that have been passed down like family heirlooms, with no one courageous and willing to say, 'enough is enough.'" — Dr. Jermaine McCalpain

This statement confronts us with a truth many people avoid. We often carry dysfunction like family treasures, even though it continues to disrupt every area of our lives.

The belief in generational curses is deeply rooted in Caribbean culture, but in many cases, it becomes a barrier to healing, a way of excusing destructive behaviours instead of examining them.

What We Call a Curse Is Often Unaddressed Trauma

Adding to Dr. McCalpain's statement, I believe a generational curse is simply: The cumulative effect of years of dysfunctional behaviours and beliefs passed down through the family line. Families unknowingly inherit emotional baggage because no intervention has ever taken place. No one has provided new information, challenged the pattern, or modeled healthier behaviour.

A significant portion of what we call "curses" is rooted not in spiritual forces, but in:

- superstition
- fear
- unhealed trauma
- misinformation
- and faulty assumptions about human behaviour

Healing begins when someone is willing to say, "Enough is enough," and then actively seek new information, new habits, and new ways of relating.

Reflection Questions

1. Which family patterns have I accepted as "just how we are"?
2. What does it mean for me to say, "Enough is enough"?
3. Who can I invite into my healing process?

Lessons from Chapter One

1. Generational curses are sometimes dysfunctional behaviours that we fail to address. These unchecked behaviours then become inhibitors to the progress of the people that come after.

2. There is power in words, they have the power of life or death. We must watch the way we speak to each other because words help to shape our destiny.

3. Dysfunctional behaviours can only be addressed when people are willing to take responsibility for their actions.

4. For change to take place, it may require someone to initiate the process.

5. Breaking the glasshouse may necessitate dealing with past hurt and pain. It will be uncomfortable, but the benefits far outweigh the discomfort.

Chapter Two

Word Power

The Language that Shapes Dysfunction

Perhaps the strongest cause of dysfunction within families is not violence, poverty, or even neglect, it is the language we use with one another. I did not fully understand until adulthood how deeply this played out in my own life. Growing up in my extended family, kind words were rare. Encouragement was nearly nonexistent. Most conversations carried a sharp edge; tones laced with criticism, sarcasm, ridicule, or anger.

Sadly, this isn't unique to my family. It's a destructive trait common across many Caribbean homes, regardless of class or background. When I began tracing my family's history, I realized this pattern wasn't new. It had been passed down for generations, spoken language shaped by frustration, silence, and survival. My grandparents, parents, aunts, and uncles all inherited this communication style, and we, in turn, became their by-products.

The good news is that more people in my generation are recognizing how harmful this has been. Some are deliberately unlearning the habits that have caused so much pain. Still, one truth remains: until families embrace the art of healthy, life-giving conversation, the cycle of dysfunction will continue.

The Power of Words to Shape Identity

I learned very early in life that words carry a power far greater than most of us realize. They can build you into a strong, confident person, or they can strip you of self-worth until you feel discarded. In the Caribbean, words are rarely neutral, we use them to stir emotion, for good or for harm. Nowhere is this more evident than in the home, where hurtful words often leave scars that never fade.

I still remember the day my grandfather called me the *"black sheep"* of the family. I was only twelve and didn't understand what it meant, but something inside me knew it wasn't good. That label stuck. For years I carried it silently, replaying the moment in my mind. Even without knowing its meaning, I absorbed it until I began to act the part. That's the danger of words; they don't just describe us; they can define us.

Affirmation in the Midst of Negativity

Apart from my parents, I rarely heard words of encouragement in my extended family. Looking back, I realize how difficult that must have been for them. Few had ever spoken words of hope into their lives, yet they chose to speak life into ours. I will always admire their courage to go against the grain of dysfunction in their own families.

Ironically, I was branded the *"black sheep"* right after passing my Common Entrance Examination to Knox College (high school placement exams), a moment that should have been celebrated. Instead, it filled me with doubt about my worth. Yet, my parents stood their ground. They deliberately distanced themselves from the toxic communication that surrounded them and chose to speak life into their children. Their words became a lifeline that helped me, and my siblings make the decision to end the cycle of dysfunction.

True change begins when we find the courage to rewrite our family narrative. In my own life, that meant learning to speak differently. My wife, Racquel, has been instrumental in this journey, teaching me the value of calm, honest, and constructive dialogue.

Words carry power, they can heal or they can harm. Real transformation begins with self-awareness. We must ask: *How do my words affect the people around me?* Too often, we perpetuate dysfunction by wounding others with the same words that once wounded us.

Breaking the "Tit-for-Tat" Cycle

This *"tit-for-tat mentality"* is something we, as Caribbean people, have perfected. But excellence in tearing each other down is not a badge of honour, it's a habit we must unlearn. To shatter the glasshouse of dysfunction, we must change how we communicate with one another.

Growing up, I saw people talking *at* each other, not *to* each other. The difference may seem small, but it's life-changing. Healing begins when our words are guided by love, understanding, and affirmation. Whether speaking to children or adults, our words should build, inspire, and offer hope for better days.

The Destructive Normalization of Verbal Abuse

Ask anyone who has walked through brokenness, and they'll tell you; negative words shape how we see ourselves. Yet, many families continue to normalize verbal abuse, name-calling, and ridicule. Words can be like missiles, once released, they leave destruction in their path, scarring hearts and reinforcing dysfunction.

Word Power: Another Perspective

Relearning How to Speak to One Another

To break the glasshouse of dysfunction, we must start by re-examining the way we speak to one another. Growing up, I often saw people talking *at* each other rather than *to* each other. The difference may seem small, but it's the difference between conflict and connection. Real transformation begins when our conversations are guided by affirmation, love, and respect.

Whether speaking to children or adults, our words should uplift, motivate, and offer hope for brighter days. Many who have endured brokenness will admit that negative words shaped how they saw themselves. Sadly, in too many homes, tearing each other down has become normal. Like missiles, careless words destroy trust, scar hearts, and keep dysfunction alive.

The Lasting Power of Words

Here are a few powerful reminders about the influence of our words:

1. "Be careful with your words. Once they are said, they can be only forgiven, not forgotten." – *Unknown*
2. "One kind word can change someone's entire day." – *Unknown*

3. "Handle them carefully, for words have more power than atom bombs." – *Pearl Strachan Hurd*

4. "Words have energy and power—with the ability to help, heal, hinder, hurt, harm, humiliate, or humble." – *Yehuda Berg*

5. "Your words have power. Speak words that are kind, loving, positive, uplifting, encouraging, and life-giving." – *Unknown*

Building a New Culture of Communication

These reminders challenge us to take responsibility for the atmosphere we create with our words. When we speak with gentleness and understanding, we invite peace into our homes. When we choose harshness, we reopen old wounds and teach the next generation to do the same.

Learning to speak differently is not easy, but it begins with awareness. It means pausing before reacting, choosing empathy over ego, and reminding ourselves that silence is sometimes more healing than speech. We cannot control how others talk to us, but we can control how we respond. Each time we choose grace over anger, we weaken the power of dysfunction.

What the Bible has to say

The Tongue: A Small Organ with Great Power

If anyone ever doubts the power of words, the Bible offers undeniable wisdom. In James 3:1–12, we are reminded that the tongue, the instrument through which words are spoken can be both a source of good and of evil. James describes how difficult it is to tame the tongue, urging us to guard our speech carefully. Proverbs 18:21 echoes this truth, declaring that *"death and life are in the power of the tongue."* In other words, our words carry the potential either to destroy or to inspire greatness in those who hear them.

Words Reveal the Condition of the Heart

For those who still believe words do not define us, Jesus provides a sobering reminder. In Matthew 15:18, He warns that *"what comes out of the mouth proceeds from the heart, and this defiles a person."* And again, in Matthew 12:34, the Master Teacher affirms, *"Out of the abundance of the heart, the mouth speaks."* These passages highlight the destructive potential of our words, but Scripture also reminds us that words can heal, encourage, and bring life when spoken with love and truth.

Speaking with Grace and Wisdom

Writing to the Christians in Colossae about nurturing healthy relationships, Paul reminds them in Colossians 4:6: *"Let your speech always be with grace, seasoned with salt, that you may know how you ought to answer each one."* Whenever I feel tempted to speak out of frustration, anger, or hurt, I remind myself: *"If it doesn't sound right in your head, it's probably better left unsaid."*

The Healing Power of Kind Words

Words have the power to bring harmony and restore joy to souls weighed down by life. Proverbs 16:24 reinforces this truth: *"Kind words are like honey—sweet to the soul and healthy for the body."* Such passages remind us that our speech can either wound or heal, and they challenge us to choose words that uplift and strengthen those around us.

Words That Transform Lives

Words are powerful tools for building people up. Lives have been transformed simply because someone spoke a kind, encouraging word. I've seen children who once walked with drooping shoulders now stand tall because someone reminded them of their worth. I've watched husbands and wives soften into each other's arms, moved by words of love and affirmation whispered in the right moment. I've seen people who never believed in their own potential take flight because someone reminded them that they have a purpose.

Choosing Life Over Death

Yes, my friend, words carry the power of life and death. One of the most effective ways to break the cycle of dysfunction is to choose life over death, starting with the words we speak.

Reflection: The Power of Words

1. How have the words spoken over my life, whether positive or negative, shaped how I see myself today?
2. Consider moments when words build you up or broke you down. What patterns do you notice in your family's language?
3. What steps can I take to change the way I speak to my loved ones?
4. Think about how you can replace criticism with encouragement, silence with affirmation, and anger with grace.
5. Who in my family needs to hear life-giving words from me today?
6. Sometimes, one conversation can begin the healing process that generations have waited for.

Lessons from Chapter Two

1. Words can shape identity, build confidence or destroy self-worth.
2. Negative labels stick; children often grow into the names spoken over them.
3. Dysfunctional communication is learned; we speak how our families spoke to us.
4. Silence hurts too. A lack of affirmation can wound just as deeply as harsh words.
5. Harsh speech is not strength, it is inherited survival behaviour, not healthy communication.
6. Words influence behaviour; they become the lens through which we see ourselves.
7. Healing begins with self-awareness; we must recognize and unlearn toxic speech patterns.
8. Changing how we speak breaks cycles; gentle, intentional communication rewrites family culture.
9. The Bible affirms word power. Scripture teaches that life and death flow from the tongue.
10. Words set the emotional climate; they determine whether homes feel safe or hostile.

Chapter Three

When is it enough?

Recognizing When the Cycle Must Break

Taking Responsibility for Our Own Choices

I believe that breaking the cycle of dysfunctional behaviour begins with taking responsibility for our own actions. As a parent, I cannot place the blame on my parents for the way I choose to interact with my child. While the way I was raised may have shaped my negative tendencies, the responsibility for my choices ultimately rests on my shoulders. Too often, we hide behind the excuse, *"Ah, just suh mi stay"*, as if our past permanently dictates our present and future. But I've come to realize that an unchanged mindset is nothing more than slavery to one's experiences, and it robs us of the possibility of change.

I had to unlearn destructive patterns, because if I had accepted *"Ah just suh mi stay"* as my truth, my life would have been very different. I would not have a joyful marriage spanning more than sixteen years. I would not have a son who I love deeply, and I certainly would not stand before audiences speaking about purpose, healing, and abundant living. The fact that I am here today is because I decided, *enough is enough.*

The Power of a Deliberate Choice

Breaking the cycle of dysfunction requires intentionality. My siblings and I refused to relive our parents' pain, so we chose to shatter the glasshouse and start again. That choice was not glamorous. It required hard, uncomfortable conversations that forced us to confront our own wounds and the ways those wounds shaped who we had become. You cannot move forward until you are willing to look backward.

Healing is a journey that requires the participation of the entire family. One person may start the conversation, but lasting change demands collective courage. Dysfunction thrives in silence and secrecy. Healing thrives in honesty and unity.

The Painful Patterns We Learned

In our family, we were never good at expressing our emotions. I love my parents dearly, but I cannot remember them having a conversation that did not end in a conflict or quarrel. I don't recall them having light moments of affectionate discourse. If I think about it, I must admit that I have never heard them express love for each other. I believe this is one of the contributing factors to my suspicions about love in my younger years.

My parents' idea of a conversation was often yelling at each other for every indiscretion or infraction. This would serve as the foundation for many of my adult relationships. I was unaware I was continuing the dysfunctional behaviours I had learned from them. It was not until my sister pointed out that we were in danger of becoming our parents that we realized how much we needed to change direction.

The Catalyst for Change

So, my sister is the catalyst for the change that we needed in our family. She is the one who started the conversation, which would eventually lead to our healing. We had to dig deep into our family history to unearth some behaviours we needed to address. We had to ask questions that sometimes could not be answered, whether out of fear or reluctance, but asking them made us aware of the issues. The people who did us wrong had to be forgiven. We had to accept that our parents did the best they could with the information they had.

It sounds weird, but I have come to terms with the fact that my grandparents were doing what they thought was best, even though sometimes their actions were outright unloving and uncaring. I realize they were only doing what they were taught. Remember what I said before? We can only make do with the information that we have. We can overcome our dysfunction because we have more information at our disposal than the people before us. Therefore, our choices can be different, and by making better choices, we can have better results.

The Psychology of "Enough Is Enough"

Coming to the point of saying "enough is enough" is often where true transformation begins. But change does not happen simply because we desire it. It requires more than willpower; it requires understanding our emotional and psychological wiring.

Each of us is shaped by:

- the patterns we observed,
- the words spoken to us,
- the conflicts we witnessed, and
- the beliefs we inherited.

Before we can transform our families, we must understand the psychology of change, how thought patterns are formed, how belief systems take root, and how they can be renewed.

Only then can we break the chains of dysfunction and build healthier, more loving family legacies.

The Psychology of Change

Recognizing the Need for Change

Several experts agree that meaningful transformation in dysfunctional families begins with two essential steps: identifying harmful behaviours and committing to change. For a family to move forward, destructive relational patterns must be broken and replaced with healthier ways of thinking and interacting.

Li (2022) emphasizes a difficult but liberating truth: We cannot change other people; we can only change ourselves. As much as we may hope otherwise, some individuals have no intention of changing or even acknowledging their toxic behaviours. In such cases, the healthiest option is to focus on our own growth and protect our peace of mind.

Why We Cannot Do It Alone

One of the biggest mistakes we make when dealing with family dysfunction is assuming we can fix everything on our own. The desire for change is admirable, but dysfunction often runs deep, panning decades or even generations. Trying to untangle these layers alone can feel like trying to push a boulder uphill.

Many of us find ourselves fighting two battles at once:

1. Making sense of our own pain, and
2. Trying to navigate the behaviours of others who are still contributing to the dysfunction.

This dual responsibility can quickly become overwhelming. Instead of drowning under the weight of unresolved trauma, the wiser choice is to seek support from trained professionals who can offer clarity, structure, and emotional protection.

The Role of Therapy in Breaking Cycles

Li (2022) offers a critical perspective: sometimes the only way to begin healing from a dysfunctional family is to work with a therapist in adulthood. Professional counselling provides a safe space to:

- process emotions,
- uncover the root causes of patterns,
- understand the deeper impact of childhood wounds, and
- learn practical tools to break free from cycles of chaos, manipulation, or neglect.

A therapist equips us with skills our family may never have modeled, such as emotional regulation, boundary setting, self-compassion, and healthy communication.

For many people, therapy becomes the turning point that allows them to envision a different kind of life.

When Healing Requires Distance

We must also face the reality that **not everyone will heal**, and not every relationship can be repaired. There are times when family patterns are so toxic that the healthiest—and sometimes only, option is to create distance. This can be painful, especially in cultures where family loyalty is expected at all costs. But separation does not mean hatred or disrespect; it often means survival. Therapy can help us navigate this painful process with wisdom and emotional support, ensuring we build healthy networks around us instead of moving forward alone.

The Cultural Barriers to Change

Understanding the psychology of change is one thing; living it out within Caribbean culture is another. Even when we recognize that something is wrong, the weight of our upbringing, community expectations, and cultural norms often keeps us stuck.

Pride, secrecy, fear, and stigma all play powerful roles.

We tell ourselves,

- *"Family business must stay in the family."*
- *"Dem ago laugh afta yuh if yuh seek help."*
- *"Strong people handle their problems alone."*

But these beliefs keep us trapped in cycles of silence and pain.

Breaking the Silence: Facing Our Reality

Why We Resist Professional Help

Although awareness about mental health is slowly improving, many Caribbean people still hesitate to seek help when dealing with emotional struggles or family dysfunction. This hesitation is rooted in decades of cultural conditioning. Traditionally, mental health professionals were viewed with suspicion, seen as meddlers, not helpers. We were taught that strength meant fixing our problems alone, and that vulnerability was weakness. As a result, many families are still suffering unnecessarily.

The Stigma Still Holding Us Back

In Jamaica, and across the Caribbean, the belief persists that visiting a counsellor or psychologist means you are "mad," "crazy," or "not right in the head." This damaging misconception has robbed countless people of the healing they desperately need.

Adding to this challenge is the deep spiritual culture of the region. Too often:

- Some turn to the *obeah man* or *reader woman* for answers.
- Others try to "pray it away," expecting God to fix what we refuse to confront.
- Many see therapy only as a last resort, something to try when everything else has collapsed.

This mindset delays healing and allows dysfunction to pass unchallenged from generation to generation.

The Need for a Cultural Shift

Williams (2013) points out that even when clear signs of emotional distress are present, many in the Caribbean still hold negative perceptions about psychological help. This puts individuals and families at risk of carrying trauma far longer than necessary.

It is heartbreaking to watch families struggle with issues that could be resolved or eased through counselling, especially when help is so close, yet so avoided.

But there is hope. More Caribbean families are beginning to share stories of how counselling has restored communication, healed old wounds, and reshaped entire family dynamics. Their testimonies could create powerful change if openly shared.

In my own family, we are not where we want to be yet—but step by step, we are moving in the right direction. Our hearts are more open. Our minds are more willing. And progress, however slow, is still progress.

Reflective Questions

1. What beliefs or fears might be keeping me from seeking help or opening up about my struggles?
2. How has my culture shaped the way I view counselling or therapy?
3. What steps can I take to make mental and emotional healing a normal part of my family's story?

Lessons from Chapter Three

1. Breaking the dysfunctional cycle starts with taking responsibility for our dysfunctional behaviours.
2. Making excuses will keep us spinning out of control in this dysfunctional cycle.
3. Sometimes we must seek the help of a trained professional to start addressing dysfunctional behaviours.
4. Addressing dysfunctional behaviours is mostly for our healing. Even if nobody else seeks help, we must seek it for ourselves.
5. Seeking help requires us to put away our biases or the stigma associated with mental health.
6. There is no shame in seeking help from a mental health professional. Dysfunctional behaviours are just challenges we need help to get over.

Chapter Four

Behind Closed Doors

The Cost of Family Secrets

The Day Silence Spoke Louder Than Words

The day I first stumbled upon a family secret; I learned that silence can shout louder than words. I remember the hushed tones, the shifting eyes, and the unspoken rule that *"we don't talk about that."* It was in that moment I realized that in my family, truth was not forbidden, it was simply buried. That experience awakened me to a deeper reality: the things we hide can shape us just as powerfully as the things we say.

The Silent Code in Dysfunctional Families

A cloak of silence is a defining feature of many dysfunctional families. Painful truths and uncomfortable topics are often swept aside and left unspoken around the family table. While every family has secrets, in dysfunctional families these secrets carry heavier and more destructive consequences.

Secrets are often held out of:

- misplaced loyalty,

- fear of conflict,
- embarrassment,
- shame, or
- a desire to protect the family name.

But instead of shielding the family, secrets often become emotional time bombs. When buried truths finally surface, and they always do, the fallout can be devastating.

The Illusion of Protection

In dysfunctional families, we learn to navigate life carefully, as if walking through a maze, always aware that the secrets we guard can erupt at any moment. Even when family members believe they are protecting each other by keeping silent, these secrets tend to backfire, creating deeper wounds and unexpected consequences.

Ironically, the things we believe are well hidden are often already public knowledge. Communities watch, observe, and talk. We spend years hiding what others have already pieced together. The energy we invest in secrecy could be better spent addressing the root issues that gave rise to the secrets in the first place.

The truth is simple: What we hide rarely protects us; it imprisons us.

When Secrets Cause More Harm Than Good

What dysfunctional families often fail to recognize is that the longer secrets are kept, the more damage they inflict. Secrets breed:

- mistrust,
- confusion,
- fractured relationships,
- emotional distance,
- resentment, and

- generational dysfunction.

We must ask ourselves honestly: Has hiding the truth ever healed a family? Has it ever solved a problem or repaired a wound?

More often than not, family secrets preserve dysfunction, normalize silence, and pass emotional burdens to the next generation.

The Pain of Discovering the Truth Too Late

When family members learn hidden truths through gossip, whispers, or third-party conversations, it almost always leads to feelings of betrayal. People begin to question:

- "Why didn't someone tell me?"
- "Who was protecting whom?"
- "What else have they kept from me?"

These questions create emotional cracks that grow into lifelong distance.

People can handle much more than they are given credit, especially when the truth is approached with compassion, sincerity, and honesty. Family secrets continue to cause unnecessary harm because silence is mistaken for protection.

Breaking the Cycle of Secrecy

Maintaining open lines of communication within the family reduces the need for secrets and builds trust. Without honest communication, distrust becomes a constant shadow. Broken relationships linger, resentment hardens, and healing becomes nearly impossible.

Breaking the cycle requires:

1. Courage to Confront the Truth

Facing uncomfortable realities is not easy, but it is necessary for growth.

2. Willingness to Speak with Love, Not Accusation
Truth spoken harshly creates arguments. Truth spoken gently creates healing.

3. Commitment to Transparency
Families heal when members feel safe enough to be honest without fear of judgment.

4. Understanding That Silence Is Not Peace
Many families confuse silence with harmony, but silence simply delays the eruption.

5. Acceptance That Healing Requires Truth
We cannot heal what we refuse to acknowledge.

The Path Forward

If we hope to break generational cycles of dysfunction, we must confront the culture of silence that has shaped our families. Secrets kept in the dark cause deeper wounds than truths brought to light. Healing cannot happen behind closed doors; it begins with honesty, spoken gently, boldly, and consistently.

Families grow stronger when truth becomes a bridge rather than a barrier. And when silence gives way to transparency, the next generation finally has a chance to breathe, heal, and begin anew.

Family secrets and dysfunctional families

Why Secrets Thrive in Dysfunctional Homes

Clinical social worker Peter K. Gerlach (2015) notes that family secrets are extremely common in dysfunctional families and often span several generations. These secrets can originate from events that are frightening, shameful, or illegal, or from personality traits considered embarrassing or unacceptable within the family. The familiar mantra, *"we don't talk about that,"* becomes a shield, one that hides reality rather than protects the family from harm.

Behaviours such as lying "to protect" others, rewriting events, or avoiding uncomfortable truths are often passed down unconsciously. Over time, these habits become deeply ingrained and continue reinforcing dysfunction. Many families fail to recognize the destructive impact of secrecy simply because it has become normal.

Writing this book forced me to confront uncomfortable truths about my own family and the dysfunction that silently shaped us. The more I explored the psychology behind secrecy, the more I understood the damage it can cause, especially when these secrets are carried from one generation to the next. If no one pauses to examine these patterns, the harm can become irreversible.

How Generational Secrets Are Passed Down

Generational secrets are not always intentional; sometimes they are embedded so deeply in a family's operating system that no one recognizes them as harmful. Below are four common ways these secrets take root and continue through generations:

1. **Secrets of Omission:** Avoiding difficult conversations or pretending certain events never happened. Example**:** Someone stops attending family gatherings, and no explanation is given.
2. **Secrets of Intention:** Creating alternate stories to hide the truth. Example: Adjusting timelines or rewriting events to protect someone's reputation.

3. **Secrets of Tradition:** Teaching children that certain topics must never be discussed. Example: "We don't talk about that in this family."

4. **Secrets of Selective Unawareness:** Choosing not to acknowledge painful truths. Example: Ignoring obvious signs of abuse or addiction in order to "keep the peace."

I witnessed all of these firsthand. Now, in midlife, I am finally beginning to understand why my family members behaved the way they did. I've learned that broken people cannot begin the journey of healing until they have acknowledged their brokenness.

The Illusion of Protection

In my family, secrets were kept with the intention of shielding us from pain. Like many Caribbean families, we lived by the rule: *"Don't air your dirty linen in public."* But silence did not spare us. If anything, it created confusion, bitterness, and misunderstanding.

Looking back, I know that if someone had gently explained the truth to me earlier, I might have made wiser decisions. Instead, the secrets I carried only added to the chaos and uncertainty in my mind. Secrets do not stop dysfunction, they strengthen it.

The Psychological Cost of Silence

Family secrets intensify psychological trauma. They act as hidden barriers that prevent:

- emotional peace
- healing
- self-understanding
- healthy relationships
- trust

- communication

Left unaddressed, secrets create fear and apprehension that ripple across generations. They burden individuals with shame and guilt, keeping them trapped in cycles of dysfunction. Ironically, the very truths being hidden are often the key to liberation and healing.

When secrets become a source of harm rather than protection, families must adopt a different approach, one that brings brokenness into the light where it can be acknowledged, addressed, and healed.

How Secrets Disrupt Family Dynamics

In his 2008 lecture on Family Systems Theory, Dan Zink identifies several ways secrets destabilize families:

1. Secrets Divide

They create invisible walls. Those kept in the dark feel excluded, suspicious, and emotionally distant.

2. Secrets Distort Perception

Half-truths lead to confusion. Without a full story, people often fill in the blanks incorrectly, resulting in misunderstandings and mistrust.

3. Secrets Block Communication

Even when family members desire closeness, secrecy keeps relationships stagnant. True intimacy cannot exist where truth is withheld.

Secrets are one of the greatest enemies of healthy family life.

Unmasking the Silence: Our Path to Freedom

As we grow in awareness, my siblings and I have become more committed to breaking the destructive cycle of secrecy in our family. Having lived through the harmful effects of hidden truths, we are determined to create a healthier path for our children and future generations.

Today's younger generation is more open, more connected, and far more willing to confront uncomfortable truths. They are unafraid to ask questions, challenge old patterns, and pursue healing. They have inspired us to do the same.

Our desire to live abundantly leaves no room for hiding truths under the illusion of protection. We refuse to maintain family traditions that demand silence at the cost of emotional and mental well-being. We understand now that protecting the family name while allowing the vulnerable to suffer is not love, it is bondage.

So we have chosen to "pull back the curtain." We are exposing painful realities, acknowledging buried wounds, and embracing the courage required for healing. As we confront our own secrets, we give others permission to confront theirs, creating a ripple effect of healing across generations.

Truth Doesn't Destroy Families—Secrecy Does

Healing begins when silence is replaced with honesty and fear is replaced with compassion. Pulling back the curtain is not easy, but the freedom that follows is worth every difficult step. When we face the painful truths of the past, we open the door to emotional restoration, for ourselves, for our families, and for the generations yet to come.

Reflection Questions

1. When was the first time I realized my family was keeping secrets? How did it make me feel?
2. Have I ever kept a secret out of fear or a desire to protect someone? What was the result?
3. What truths in my family might need to be brought into the light for healing to begin?
4. How can I practice truth-telling with love rather than anger or shame?
5. What might freedom look like for me if I stopped carrying someone else's silence?

Lessons from Chapter Four

1. A veil of secrecy does little to help dysfunctional behaviour in the family.
2. The secrets we try to protect are usually known by people who can do nothing to help.
3. Keeping secrets allows psychological trauma to increase over time.
4. It requires courage to expose harmful secrets, but it pays off in the end.
5. Keeping secrets helps to strengthen the positions of wrongdoers in the family.
6. Keeping secrets is one of the greatest barriers to effective communication in families.
7. Secrets can have devastating consequences that can impact several generations in the family.

Chapter Five

My Black is Beautiful:

Healing from the Shades of Dysfunction

"Nutten too black, nuh good." Those words, repeated by some of my relatives, carried more power than they ever realized. Behind that phrase lived a painful belief that lighter skin meant greater worth. This mindset, rooted in colourism, runs deep within Caribbean families, shaping how generations see themselves and each other. It is a silent destroyer, teaching children that beauty and value are measured in shades of brown.

Growing up, I lived this reality. Among my siblings, I was the darkest. My father's family had a mix of light and dark skin tones, as did my mother's. From a young age, I was reminded, subtly and sometimes directly, that "fairer" was better. My grandparents carried a plantation-era mentality, a mindset inherited from colonial oppression. My grandmother didn't hesitate to warn me that if I wanted to succeed, I would have to "outshine" others because I was "too black."

I loved my grandparents, but they carried wounds that had been handed down to them, destructive beliefs disguised as wisdom. They spoke with conviction, not malice, yet their words shaped me in ways they could not have imagined. When a child is told, directly or indirectly, that their worth depends on their skin tone, the wound runs deep. It takes years, sometimes decades, to heal.

For a long time, I struggled with identity. I was not only fighting the colourism in my family but also the version I had internalized. When you begin to see yourself through the eyes of others, it takes extraordinary courage to rediscover who God says you are. Through faith, love, and time, I found my worth, not in complexion but in purpose.

When a child is told they are unworthy of acceptance, it sets them up for a life of struggle, missed opportunities, and self-doubt, unless someone intervenes. In my case, I was fortunate that, as an adult, I received the guidance and intervention that helped me discover my purpose and unlock my potential.

I refused to accept that my destiny was to become just another statistic. Though it took time to find my path, I eventually discovered my true worth. Yes, my family was dysfunctional and broken, but I was determined not to let that define my reality or that of my siblings.

We chose to do things differently, and today we are seeing the positive impact in our children's lives. We could have given up and followed a path of self-destruction, but that would have condemned another generation to the same dysfunction we endured as children.

If the glasshouse is to be shattered, families must understand that the choice to live better lives rests in their hands. We cannot continue to blame those who came before us for our current circumstances because we have the power to choose differently.

Colourism and the Dysfunctional Family

Colourism doesn't just divide communities; it fractures families. It creates quiet rivalries, subtle resentments, and deep insecurities that travel across generations. In the Caribbean, where the echoes of colonial rule still linger, these divisions often hide beneath jokes, compliments, and casual remarks, but their effects are anything but harmless.

Colourism is the cultural preference for lighter skin over darker skin. Unfortunately, in the Caribbean, we are still a far way from fully embracing our Afro-centric roots. While people rarely express outright dislike for darker skin, the subtle messages are unmistakable.

Our colonial history, which promoted the idea that "white is right," has left lasting effects. Many families, consciously or unconsciously, pass these beliefs down from one generation to the next. Even today, the struggle with skin tone persists, continuing to reinforce cycles of dysfunction within families.

Here is an example of the colourism being referred to in an article written by Kizanne James in September 2020:

L (from the Bahamas), "My experience with colourism began as a child before I knew the meaning of the word or understood the concept. I would often hear my grandmother call other kids "dark," "black like tar," and "dirty." In my mind, dark-skinned became synonymous with dirty, something I didn't want to be. As such, my daily routine included scrubbing my face, arms, and legs, sometimes until the skin came off, just to get that light "clean" look.

My cousins, who were a darker shade than I, were treated differently. They were called last for dinner and often denied candy and treats.

What's worse is that they knew they were left out because they weren't "pretty." I had other cousins who were of a lighter hue than I was, and they were treated as royalty when they came to visit my grandmother's house. They got the best food and ate out of the "good" dishware. In her eyes, they were special and could do nothing wrong.

L's story reflects the experience of many children and adults in the Caribbean. From an early age, notions of colourism are planted in young minds, causing some to resent siblings or cousins, while others develop feelings of superiority because they are told they have a "high complexion." These early messages can lead to low self-esteem for some, or arrogance and self-centeredness for others, patterns that often persist into adulthood.

Breaking this cycle requires intentional effort and conscious choices, but sadly, it often feels like an uphill battle against deeply ingrained cultural norms.

I have witnessed this dysfunctional behaviour firsthand, and it still exists on both sides of my family. While it is rarely discussed at family gatherings, anyone who observes closely and listens carefully will notice it. I have met friends and even family members who dread these gatherings because they feel like Cinderella, the uninvited stepsister.

This expression of colourism may not be intentional, but it is deeply ingrained. Passed down through generations, it has become so embedded in our family DNA that we often continue the behaviour unconsciously, rarely pausing to consider where it originated.

L's story could easily have been my own — or that of many others across the Caribbean. From a young age, these messages shaped our sense of belonging. Those praised for being "brownin'" grow up with pride that can turn to arrogance, while those labeled "too black" carry shame that becomes self-doubt. Both sides of the colour spectrum lose. Healing begins only when we acknowledge the damage and choose to unlearn what we've inherited.

Reflection Questions

1. What early messages shaped how I view my own skin or beauty?
2. How have I seen colourism affect relationships in my family or community?
3. Have I ever been guilty of reinforcing colour-based biases, even unconsciously?
4. What would it look like to affirm the beauty of every shade in my family?
5. How can I help the next generation see themselves through God's eyes rather than society's?

Lessons from Chapter Five

1. Discrimination based on skin tone is a feature of dysfunctional families.
2. Many people grow up despising their sense of self because of how they were treated because of their skin colour.
3. Our strong connections to slavery have led us to dismiss the idea that there is beauty in blackness.
4. Colourism is a feature of many Caribbean societies.
5. Discrimination based on colour is unconsciously passed down through generations.
6. Overcoming the effects of colourism requires education and action on the part of families who desire change.

Chapter Six

Redefining Normal

When Chaos Feels Comfortable

For years, I mistook chaos for closeness. We must be careful not to confuse dysfunctional behaviour with normal family life. When certain patterns repeat long enough, they begin to feel ordinary, even acceptable. Looking back, I now realize that many things we considered "just the way we are" were, in fact, deeply dysfunctional.

In our home, any disagreement could quickly turn into a shouting match. Arguments often dragged in old grudges and unresolved pain. Even the children were drawn in, choosing sides to defend the adults they loved. At the time, it felt natural almost like proof of loyalty. But in truth, that environment was shaping us in ways none of us fully understood.

Learning the Difference

Healthy families are not perfect, but they communicate with care. They argue, but they do so with respect and love. Dysfunctional families, on the other hand, normalize behaviour that damages hearts and relationships.

In a healthy family:

- Communication builds rather than breaks.
- Conflicts are resolved respectfully and fairly.
- Everyone feels safe, valued, and heard.

In a dysfunctional family:

- Arguments escalate quickly and drag in the past.
- Children are forced to pick sides.
- Emotional safety is replaced by fear or silence.

When we begin to mistake this kind of environment for normal, we lose sight of what healthy love looks like.

The Weight of Dysfunction

Family dysfunction is like a slow poison it dulls the spirit and reshapes your idea of love. I know, because I lived it.

Growing up, Saturday mornings were the hardest. After we moved back to the country to live with our grandparents, those mornings became ritualized pain. There was no escape from the tension. We would sit quietly while our grandparents voiced their disappointment in my mother, comparing her unfavourably to her siblings. Their words were sharp, meant to teach a lesson, but they left deep scars.

My mother had been the "bright one," the one expected to lift the family's reputation. Her setbacks became a constant source of criticism. We, her children, became unwilling participants in that disappointment reminders of her "failure."

It took years for me to understand that what they saw as discipline was emotional damage in disguise.

Breaking the Habit of Hurt

The turning point for me came when I started to see my nieces and nephews interact with others. Their laughter, gentleness, and confidence showed me what healthy relationships could look like. I realized I didn't have to pass on what I had inherited. Dysfunction was not destiny it was a learned behaviour that could be unlearned.

To break free, we must first name what we see. When we call dysfunction what it truly is, we rob it of its power.

Learning What Love Looks Like

True education is not limited to books or degrees it is the process of learning how to live differently. The moment we begin to question what we once accepted as normal; we begin to heal.

Ask yourself:

- Do I feel safe being myself around my family?
- Are disagreements handled with respect or ridicule?
- Do I use words that wound or words that heal?

Awareness is the beginning of wisdom. When we know better, we can do better for ourselves, for our children, and for the generations yet to come.

Faith and a New Normal

Healing does not mean forgetting the past. It means learning from it and refusing to let it dictate our future. God has given us the power to renew our minds, to transform our homes, and to love differently. Dysfunction may have been the pattern, but it is not the promise.

We can choose to redefine normal — one conversation, one act of grace, one "I love you" at a time.

Reflection Questions

1. What patterns from my childhood did I once believe were normal?
2. How do I respond when conflict arises in my home or relationships?
3. Who in my life has shown me what healthy love looks like?
4. In what ways can I express love more openly to those around me?
5. What can I do this week to model a new normal for my family?

Lessons from Chapter Six

1. Without information and intervention, dysfunctional behaviours are accepted as normal.
2. We develop coping mechanisms to mask the effects of dysfunctional behaviour.
3. Dysfunctional behaviours, if not addressed, can lead to physical and psychological abuse.
4. Knowledge is the first step in the process of overcoming dysfunctional behaviours.
5. Conflict resolution is important to help overcome dysfunctional behaviour.

Chapter Seven

Choosing a Different Path

A New Generation, a New Beginning

As I reflect on what it means to shatter the glasshouse, I'm in awe of how far our family has come. Though we've grown from our experiences, the journey toward wholeness is still ongoing. Overcoming dysfunction in any family depends on the choices we make and often, it takes just one person to begin the process of change.

In our family, that person was my sister. She became pregnant at nineteen, and as her older brother, I was worried. After all, our mother had me at nineteen too, and I feared history was about to repeat itself. But my sister made a different choice. From the moment she discovered she was expecting, she resolved not to repeat the mistakes of the past. Her determination hit me like a ton of bricks. Watching her carve out a new path not only shaped her child's future but also inspired me to redirect my own life's course.

A Sister's Example

Watching my sister raise her children restored my hope. Given all we endured growing up, one might have expected her to continue the same dysfunctional patterns. Instead, she poured love, patience, and grace into her children.

Our parents did their best, but the environment they grew up in made it difficult for love to be expressed in healthy ways. Even when love was present, it came filtered through fear, frustration, or silence. Seeing my sister nurture her children helped me realize how much love we had missed and how much love was still possible.

Her example opened my eyes. It showed me that holding on to pain robs us of the chance to give and receive love in the present. Her courage to love differently gave me hope that our story didn't have to end in dysfunction.

Faith and a New Vision

My sister's life choices, and my own journey to faith, became turning points for our family. Before I became a Christian in 1998, I had no interest in marriage or starting a family. Like many men I knew, I accepted casual, non-committal relationships as normal. I thought avoiding attachment would protect me from disappointment.

But my faith changed everything. Through the teachings of the church, I began to understand that family is central to God's design. The church, after all, is modeled after the family. If I wanted to serve God wholeheartedly, I had to rethink my approach to relationships.

Faith taught me that love requires commitment, that fatherhood is a sacred calling, and that healing is possible only when we stop living by the world's broken patterns.

Breaking the Cycle Together

The effects of choosing differently are visible in my brothers' lives as well. I have three younger brothers, and each of them has embraced a family-oriented lifestyle that directly contradicts the dysfunction we once knew. Their commitment to raising loving, stable families is proof that generational cycles can be broken.

We no longer blame our parents or grandparents for what they could not give us. They did the best they could with what they had. Instead, we are grateful for their sacrifices and determined to build upon their lessons their successes and their mistakes to create something better.

Redefining Success

When I look at my son, nieces, and nephews, I feel an overwhelming sense of gratitude. They are well-adjusted children, enjoying life the way children should.

There was a time when I believed success meant giving my child everything I lacked, more money, more opportunities, more things. But as I matured, my focus shifted. True success is not about possessions but peace. It's about creating a home free from the emotional baggage of the past.

I can only achieve that by making conscious choices every day, by choosing to love well, to communicate honestly, and to forgive often. That is what it means to shatter the glasshouse.

Reflection Questions

1. Who in your family has inspired you to choose a different path?
2. What steps can you take today to begin breaking your family's cycle of pain or dysfunction?
3. How has unforgiveness held you back, and what might happen if you released it?
4. How does your faith inform the way you approach relationships and family life?
5. What legacy of love do you want to leave for the next generation?

Lessons from Chapter Seven

1. Change begins with one decision. One person's choice can alter an entire family's future.
2. Forgiveness is freedom. It releases the past and makes space for healing.
3. Faith reshapes perspective. God's design for family is rooted in love, not fear.
4. Dysfunction is not destiny. With courage and intention, cycles can be broken.
5. Love is the legacy. The greatest inheritance we can leave is emotional wholeness.

Chapter Eight

Behind the Façade of Family

The Illusion of Caribbean Family Unity

Many Caribbean people proudly declare themselves to be "family oriented." We boast about our close-knit communities, our willingness to "raise the village," and the strong bonds that supposedly define our culture. And yes, when a crisis hits, we show up. We defend one another fiercely, and outsiders are quick to admire our unity.

But beneath that façade of strength and togetherness lies another reality, one often marked by hurt, secrecy, jealousy, rivalry, and brokenness. In Jamaica, it is not uncommon to hear stories of domestic disputes, generational conflict, and even fatal confrontations between relatives. All of this occurs within families that appear "tight-knit" to the outside world.

When we dare to look closer, what we often interpret as unity is really a learned survival strategy. It is the way we cope, not a sign of true harmony. Under the surface, dysfunction simmers quietly, waiting for the right moment to explode. Until we acknowledge this truth, we will continue to confuse survival with strength, and pain with love.

Discipline or Dysfunction?

Rethinking Corporal Punishment

This is perhaps the most difficult section of this chapter to write because it challenges long-standing cultural norms. Many of us grew up believing that corporal punishment was the most effective form of discipline. "Floggings," "lickings," and "beatings" were treated not as harmful but as necessary, almost noble.

After years of studying counselling and psychology, I am convinced that what many Caribbean homes called *discipline* was, in fact, physical abuse.

Corporal punishment has been normalized for generations. Parents and grandparents took pride in "using the rod" because they genuinely believed it shaped children into respectful, responsible adults. But we must consider how these practices contributed to cycles of aggression, emotional withdrawal, and dysfunction, patterns that continue to influence the high rates of domestic violence in our society today.

I remember telling my mother that the beatings I received did *not* make me who I am today. They did not shape my character, my decisions, or my values as a teenager or young adult.

Too many people proudly proclaim, "A di beating mek yuh tun out good!" But the truth is that many dysfunctional adults today are the products of that same beating culture.

I am grateful for my parents; they did their best with what they knew. But some things they believed to be discipline were really harmful responses to frustration, fear, and lack of proper tools.

Beating a child into submission does not produce wisdom. It produces fear, resentment, or rebellion.

I was often beaten "in advance", punished for what I *might* do, not what I did. The more I was beaten, the more rebellious I became. What was meant to steer me toward righteousness nearly pushed me toward ruin.

I am who I am today because of positive influences, from mentors, counsellors, my wife, and the people who chose to build me rather than break me.

The High Cost of Poor Communication

Corporal punishment often becomes a substitute for genuine communication. Many parents resort to "floggings" because they lack the tools to guide their children through conversation, correction, and emotional regulation.

Healthy communication, the ability to explain right from wrong, to listen, to guide, and to affirm, was largely absent in many older generations. As a result, thousands of Caribbean adults today are emotionally wounded, unable to articulate their needs, and uncertain about how to parent differently.

I cannot recall a single moment in childhood when anyone, parent, grandparent, aunt, or uncles sat me down to explain *why* my behaviour was wrong. No one reasoned with me. No one guided me with patience or clarity. All I remember is the sting of the rod.

Fear may stop a behaviour temporarily, but it does not teach values.

Today, when I look at my son, emotionally healthy, confident, and secure, I am grateful my wife and I chose a different path. We practice constructive discipline, one rooted in explanation, boundaries, and affection.

We use consequences, yes, but never beatings.

Watching my son thrive assures me that cycles of dysfunction *can* be broken when parents choose intentional, thoughtful approaches.

What is the solution?

We cannot rewrite history, and we cannot undo the harm caused by those who believed they were doing the right thing. But we *can* chart a new course.

We must:

- **Face the truth** about the harm inflicted by certain cultural norms
- **Stop blaming the past** for our present choices
- **Take responsibility** for raising healthier families
- **Break old patterns** rather than maintain them out of loyalty
- **Choose communication over violence**
- **Parent with intention rather than tradition**

Dragging the pain of the past into the future only ensures that the next generation suffers the same fate. Shattering the glasshouse requires courage, the courage to admit the old way failed, the courage to do better, and the courage to endure the discomfort that comes with change.

Not everything our parents or grandparents did was wrong. They worked with the knowledge they had. But we have access to information, tools, and insight they did not. It would be tragic to waste this advantage by repeating history.

Breaking dysfunction is not instantaneous; it is a journey filled with setbacks and breakthroughs. But too much is at stake to quit. Future generations depend on the choices we make today. Failure is not an option. If we are going to shatter the glasshouse, we must leave the past behind and begin making deliberate choices that will finally break the cycle.

Reflection Questions

1. What messages about discipline did I inherit from my parents or community?
2. How have those lessons shaped the way I correct or relate to others?
3. What would discipline look like if love, not fear, were my guiding principle?
4. How can I begin to model healthier correction for the next generation?
5. What does it mean for me to "discipline without damaging"?

Lessons from Chapter Eight

1. If dysfunction is not addressed as time passes, we just learn how to cope with it.
2. There is a connection between high levels of domestic violence and dysfunctional behaviours in families.
3. Verbal abuse is a feature of dysfunctional behaviour among families.
4. There is a difference between physical abuse and discipline. Because of a lack of communication skills, physical abuse is frequently disguised as discipline.
5. Failure is not an option that we should be willing to accept. We must find constructive ways to curb dysfunctional behaviours.

Chapter Nine

The Turning Point:

From Brokenness to Breakthrough

A Defining Moment

June 10, 1998, marked a turning point in my life. I often tell friends that this date set me firmly on the path of passion and purpose. On that day, I was baptized and became a member of the Church of Christ. From there, I came under the guidance of a patient minister whose mentorship and genuine concern shaped the course of my life. Without his dedication, my story might have taken a very different direction. Becoming a Christian gave me a new perspective and a hope I had never known before.

I am deeply grateful for that fateful day when, through our shared love for football, God used a fellow minister to visit my home. Looking back, I see it as undeniable proof that God knows exactly what we need, when we need it, and that His will always prevails.

By 1998, years of dysfunctional behaviour had finally caught up with me. I had reached the lowest point in my life and didn't know where to turn. Professionally, financially, and personally, everything was falling apart. No matter what I tried, it seemed destined to end in disaster, and more than once, I felt like giving up on life.

I had hit rock bottom, or so I thought. Just when it seemed things couldn't possibly get worse, they did. Exhaustion and depression settled in like a heavy cloud. Some mornings I didn't even want to get out of bed to face the problems waiting for me. I felt utterly alone, with no one to confide in, and I had become skilled at hiding my pain. What I didn't realize, however, was that God was already at work preparing my rescue, sending into my life a minister, a brother in Christ, a mentor, and ultimately a friend for life.

From Chaos to Clarity

I was a lost soul, shaped by the negative experiences of my childhood as I stumbled from adolescence into adulthood. In trying to escape the dysfunction of my past, I became the very thing I feared. My life spiraled into destructive patterns with little thought for the consequences. I smoked weed, drank heavily, and lived recklessly, surrounded by more women than I could ever count.

My hard-earned money vanished as quickly as it came, poured into parties and late-night escapades. Many mornings, I would wake up in a stranger's house with no memory of how I got there. To some young men, this might sound like the dream, the life of a king, but it was empty, shallow, and far from glamorous.

A New Perspective

My new lease on life gave me a fresh perspective on everything. I had reached my breaking point; I was exhausted from waking up each day unsure of my purpose. By society's standards, my life looked enviable: I partied every weekend, had the right friends, frequented the popular spots, and possessed nearly everything a young man could desire, but I was profoundly unhappy.

There was a constant sense that something was missing, though I couldn't identify what it was. Later, during counselling as part of my master's program, I realized this restlessness and lack of fulfilment were deeply tied to my family's brokenness. I had been trying to function in a world of hurt, and the only way forward was to confront my demons head-on. Making that choice was the best decision I've ever made; it set me on the path to true healing.

The Power of Mentorship

I first met Carl Powell through my younger brother Andrew in 1997. Andrew, a devoted member of the Church of Christ, had been inviting me to attend worship for months, but I was not interested. It took a personal incident that forced me to reevaluate my life for me to finally agree to go.

That first Sunday, he invited me to a Bible study at my home. After that, he would show up every Monday at 1 p.m. for nearly a year, without fail. What struck me most was his genuine concern for me as a person. The studies were meaningful, but it was his mentorship, his care for my life, that made the difference.

Carl Powell is the person I credit with guiding me toward the answers I had been searching for and setting me on the path to transformation.

I obeyed the gospel at 2 p.m. on June 10, 1998, the same day the World Cup began, though that was the last thing on my mind. Robert Solomon, who would later become a close friend, came to my house with Carl Powell that day. After about two hours of Bible study, I was confronted with a question I could not answer. I realized in that moment that if I couldn't answer it, I needed to change the way I was living my life.

That afternoon at 2 p.m., I was baptized. From that point on, everything changed. I became part of a community that accepted me, flaws and all, and I discovered a renewed sense of hope and purpose. The first years of being a Christian were incredibly challenging, yet they were the ones that illuminated the family patterns I needed to break.

The Healing Power of God's Love

Dysfunctional relationships often leave people carrying heavy emotional baggage and a deep sense of unworthiness. Feelings of inadequacy make it difficult to give or receive love, and trust becomes a constant struggle. Many live guarded, always bracing for disappointment or betrayal. I know this reality well; it was my life before I became a Christian.

Everything shifted, however, when I discovered that God loves me unconditionally. That revelation gave me no choice but to see myself and my life through a new set of lenses.

Growing up, church on Sundays was simply part of our weekly routine. It was about attendance, not about cultivating a personal relationship with Jesus Christ. But when I truly came into a relationship with God,

I discovered the depth of what it means to be a Christian. I realized that God heals broken humanity through His unconditional love.

It wasn't until I began studying the Bible with seriousness that I saw how broken I really was, and how only God's love could mend me. Through worship, prayer, study, praise, and fellowship, a new world of love and acceptance opened before me, and the transformation I had long desired finally began.

The Bible is filled with stories of God using broken people to accomplish His purpose. His love, poured into their lives, transformed them despite their flaws. I look at people like Rahab, Abraham, and Jacob, each with their struggles and dysfunctions, and yet God still used them and sealed their destinies with His grace.

In the same way, my brokenness and failures cannot stop the love of Jesus Christ from covering my soul. This truth gives me hope: no matter my shortcomings, I am still a vessel God can use for His glory.

To know God's love is to embrace the truth of who you are without shame or fear. Before my relationship with Jesus Christ, I was afraid of facing my truth. Now, I no longer worry because no one has the authority to judge my journey. I may have come from a past filled with struggle and turmoil, but I now wear my story as a badge of honour, for it has shaped who I am.

Some people may feel uncomfortable with my openness, but I've learned that hiding only deepens the scars. God's love compels me to stand boldly in my truth, leaving others with a choice, to reject me or accept me as I am.

My Place of Refuge

When I needed to escape the ghosts of my past, the church became my place of refuge. It wasn't perfect, but compared to what I had known before, it felt like a breath of fresh air. I left home at an early age, forced to grow up quickly and make decisions I wasn't fully prepared for. Many of those choices came with painful consequences, and at times, the weight of it all left me depressed and wanted to hide from the world.

I didn't feel like I could confide in my siblings, who were facing their own struggles, and many of my friends were just as broken, battling demons of their own. But when I came to know Christ, I began laying down those burdens one by one. The walls of the glasshouse I had been trapped in started to shatter, and through the love and support of the church, I found the strength to navigate the tunnel of emotions that had once held me captive.

My new embrace of the church as a place of refuge stirred within me a deep desire to serve in ministry. I often describe the church as a sanctuary for wounded souls because that is what it was for me. In its embrace, I found renewed purpose and a reason to live again. Many others, like me, are trying to escape the painful memories of dysfunctional family life, searching for a safe place to heal. The church must always be ready to welcome such hearts and guide them into becoming faithful, fruitful citizens of God's kingdom. As a refuge, it may be the only source of hope for those battling the scars of dysfunction. If the church neglects this role, the cost will be felt not just in the present but in the brokenness of future generations.

Reflection Questions and Renewal

1. **What was my turning point?**
   Reflect on a moment when life forced you to choose between continuing in dysfunction or stepping into change. What did that moment teach you about God's timing?

2. **Who has mentored me along the way?**
   Think about the people God has placed in your path; pastors, friends, or relatives, who helped redirect your course. How can you express gratitude or pay that mentorship forward?

3. **What does unconditional love mean to me?**
   Consider how your understanding of love has changed since encountering God's grace. Are there relationships that still need healing through that same love?

4. **Where do I find refuge today?**
   Identify the space spiritual or emotional, where you feel safe and accepted. Are you creating that same refuge for others who are struggling?

5. **How can my story inspire others?**
   Every testimony carries power. How might your experiences of brokenness and transformation to guide others toward hope, faith, and healing?

Lessons from Chapter Nine

1. It takes the patience of only one person to change your perspective on life.
2. Dysfunctional behaviours will take a toll on you if there is no intervention.
3. You cannot outrun your destiny. There will come a time when you must face your demons.
4. There is no substitute for dealing with the pains of a dysfunctional family life.
5. A relationship with God is a good place to start to overcome dysfunction.
6. God places people in our lives at the right time to give us direction and purpose.

Chapter Ten

The Freedom of Forgiveness

A Choice That Changed Everything

When forgiveness is genuine, it feels as though the weight of the world has been lifted from your shoulders. I came to realize that I had been holding on to pain for far too long, pain that drained me emotionally, weighed me down physically, and nearly pushed me over the edge. Earlier, I mentioned forgiving my father for his past shortcomings. That decision was not the result of a life-changing conversation between us; it was my choice. I knew that if I was going to move forward and truly heal, forgiveness had to come from me. There are things my father cannot speak about, and I have made peace with that reality. Over the years, we have had several conversations, but my freedom did not come from his words, it came from my decision to let go.

Forgiveness as a Daily Practice

In Matthew 18:21–22, when Peter asked Jesus how many times he should forgive, the Lord replied, "as often as necessary." As a Christian, I had to learn to apply this principle not only to my father but also to others with whom I have had difficult relationships. Genuine forgiveness is not a one-time event, it is a continual practice, a daily choice. When we are truly in tune with God, we recognize that if we refuse to forgive repeatedly, we condemn ourselves to living in pain and allow dysfunction to perpetuate itself. Forgiveness is not contingent on the offender seeking it; rather, it is a gift we extend for our own healing and freedom.

Sometimes life does not give us the chance to resolve every issue with those who have hurt us. In the case of my grandparents, I never fully worked through the pain of the past, but I did experience a measure of healing with my grandfather before he died.

Reconciliation and Redemption

I am not sure if it was age, illness, or God simply softening his heart, but in his final years he became calmer and more approachable. We shared a few meaningful conversations, and though we never spoke directly about his past actions, I remember looking into his eyes and seeing what his weakened body could no longer put into words.

The same man who once branded me the *"black sheep"* of the family became my source of wisdom and quiet encouragement in his last days. One memory remains especially dear to me: before he passed away in the hospital, I was the last person to see him. Sitting by his bedside, I read Psalm 121 from his favourite Bible. As I read, he lifted his eyes to me with a look of peace and gratitude that spoke volumes. In that moment, I came full circle, I forgave the man I once could not bear to be in the same room with, and instead I left with a memory of grace and reconciliation that I will treasure for the rest of my life.

Forgiving the Unspoken

My grandmother was truly one of a kind. She carried herself with dignity, and admitting she was wrong was never part of her nature. Known for speaking her mind without hesitation, she was often misunderstood. I believe much of this stemmed from the pain she carried from her own past, pain she never quite learned to release. She was a paradox: capable of doing things that felt deeply unloving, yet also generous with acts of kindness. Having grown up in the old Jamaica, where people believed skin complexion determined one's chance at upward mobility, she openly embraced those ideas and made no effort to hide them. With my grandmother, there was little middle ground, you either loved her with all her flaws or resented her for the weight of her archaic beliefs. Unlike with my grandfather, I never had the chance to share meaningful conversations with her before she died. So, for my own healing, I chose to forgive her and love her, and in doing so, I began the work of shattering the glasshouse.

The Power of Letting Go

The fellowship of church taught me that forgiveness is a choice, and I chose to forgive, not because anyone asked me to, but for my own sanity and peace of mind. Looking back at my life and all that I have done, I sometimes feel unworthy of God's forgiveness. Yet Jesus Christ chose to die for me, freeing me from guilt and shame. Who am I not to extend that same grace, even when it requires every ounce of strength and resolve? I refuse to be a victim of my circumstances, and I will not allow an unforgiving heart to dictate how I live. True forgiveness is not about feelings; it is a deliberate act, a conscious decision. I forgive, not because I want to, but because it is necessary for me to discover my purpose and continue shattering the glasshouse on my journey.

Forgive to Heal

As we journey through life, people will inevitably wound sometimes intentionally, sometimes not. Even those closest to us can cause deep pain through their words and actions. These experiences often leave behind scars of resentment, bitterness, and anger, which can easily harden into hatred if left unchecked. Yet, when we hold on to hurt, we are the ones who suffer most. The only path to true freedom is forgiveness. Developing a heart that forgives allows us to release the pain and make room for love, peace, and hope to flourish.

Benefits of Forgiveness:

- Healthier relationships.
- Improved mental health.
- Less anxiety, stress, and hostility.
- Fewer symptoms of depression.
- Lower blood pressure.
- A stronger immune system.
- Improved heart health.
- Improved self-esteem.

Guiding Principles of Forgiveness:

1. **Forgiveness is a choice.** You can choose to forgive even if the person who committed the offence never asks for your forgiveness. When you forgive, you are choosing to let go of the anger and pain that someone has caused you.

2. **Forgiveness is a blessing.** Forgiveness adds blessings to our lives because we are carrying around the burden of hurt and pain that someone has caused us.

3. **To forgive is to forget.** Until you no longer habour in your heart the hurt others have caused, you have not truly forgiven. You can choose to free your heart from the bitterness and anger caused by someone else's actions.

4. **Forgiveness is not conditional.** You do not have to wait for an apology to forgive someone. You can forgive someone even if they don't deserve it or are not sorry for what they did.

5. **Forgiveness is the key to peace.** Forgiveness gives us peace of mind. It is hard to have inner peace when we are holding on to anger and resentment. When we forgive, we let go of those negative emotions and replace them with positive ones.

6. **Forgiveness is the key to happiness.** If we still have resentment and anger in us, we can never find true happiness in life.

7. **Forgiveness Heals.** Forgiveness has the power to heal our broken hearts and relationships. It can mend the rift that was caused by anger and resentment.

8. **Forgiveness is the foundation of love.** Love cannot grow in an environment of unforgiveness. Unforgiveness will only breed more anger, resentment, and bitterness. If we want to experience true love, we need to forgive.

   (https://triviafaithblog.com/the-power-of-forgiveness/)

Reflection & Renewal

1. Who in my life have I held in the prison of unforgiveness?
2. What emotions do I still carry from past wounds that need release?
3. How does forgiving others bring me closer to understanding God's grace?
4. In what ways has forgiveness freed me to live with peace and purpose?
5. How can I model forgiveness within my family to help shatter cycles of dysfunction?

Lessons from Chapter Ten

1. Letting go of hurt and pain will help the healing begin.
2. Forgiveness is a choice, but it is a choice that is worth it.
3. Genuine forgiveness has its foundation in God's word.
4. To protect your soul, be willing to forgive those who are no longer alive.
5. When you find it hard to forgive, remember that God forgave you and commands that you learn to forgive others.
6. Forgiveness is a process, and you must take time to work through the steps.

Chapter Eleven

Confronting to Heal

Facing the Uncomfortable Truth

In Matthew 5:22–24, Jesus teaches a vital truth: confronting problems is often the first step toward resolving them. Many of us avoid confrontation because it exposes our vulnerabilities yet avoiding it only allows dysfunction to deepen.

One major reason families remain trapped in cycles of pain is the fear that revisiting the past will reopen old wounds. Instead of addressing our issues, we bury them beneath silence and denial. I once believed that avoiding confrontation was the same as keeping the peace. But peace built on silence is fragile, it cracks under the weight of unspoken pain.

The church helped me develop problem-solving skills to face my family's dysfunction head-on, and one of the most powerful among them is *healthy confrontation.* When done with love and humility, confrontation does not create hatred or deepen pain opens the door to healing. True restoration cannot happen without confrontation, but it must be *constructive*, not destructive.

Confront the Problem, Not the Person

One of the most important lessons I've learned in dealing with dysfunctional behaviour is this: confront the *problem*, not the *person*. The goal is always healing, not hurting.

This begins with honesty, acknowledging your emotions before speaking. If confrontation will only stir up anger or lead to conflict, it's wiser to wait until you can approach the situation calmly and prayerfully. Often, people's behaviour is not a reflection of cruelty or indifference but of their own unresolved pain.

Understanding this allows us to respond with compassion instead of resentment. When we seek to uncover the reasons behind someone's dysfunction, we position ourselves to address the issue more effectively. But if we fight fire with fire, we only fuel the same destructive cycle we are trying to break.

The Necessity of Vulnerability

The church taught me that running away from problems only delays the inevitable, they always find their way back. Most families avoid facing the uncomfortable truth that years of buried emotions must eventually be unearthed.

Vulnerability is frightening because it means exposing the secrets we've spent a lifetime hiding. Yet, if future generations are to live freer and healthier lives, we must confront the pain of the past and let healing begin. Working through family issues is never easy, but it is essential for survival and growth.

I've made a personal commitment to apply the biblical principles I've learned in the church to help bring healing to my family. This, I believe, is my greatest contribution to *shattering the glasshouse.*

Acceptance and the Power of Letting Go

There are certain realities in life that we simply must learn to accept. In a perfect world, everything would unfold according to our plans, but life rarely works that way. We must learn to accept people and situations as they are, or we set ourselves up for continual disappointment.

Coming to terms with certain truths about my family has brought me peace. I've realized that I cannot change anyone. This doesn't mean I accept dysfunctional behaviour as normal; it means I understand that true change only happens when a person is willing. No matter how sincere our intentions may be, healing will always be difficult if the family itself is not ready to heal.

The church has also taught me that another person's inappropriate behaviour should never dictate how I respond to them. My reactions are now guided by a deeper desire, to please God in every situation.

Acceptance reminds me that I always have the power of choice. To some, letting go of the baggage of dysfunction might seem like taking the easy way out, but I've learned that the harder road is often the one that leads to peace. There's no victory in constantly swimming against the current; sometimes, wisdom means accepting what is, releasing what was, and moving forward in faith.

When Escape Isn't the Answer

I grew up in a home marked by constant fights, quarrels, and tension—times when our parents' disappointments made us feel like outsiders in our own family. Those experiences left deep scars. Though there were moments of joy in my childhood, I would trade many of them not to have lived through the trauma that shaped me.

So, when the first chance to escape came, I took it, believing distance would solve everything. But life has a way of confronting us with the very things we try hardest to forget, and when it does, there's no hiding.

In my search for a fresh start, I found refuge in the church a sanctuary for the broken and weary. Like the lost souls in Luke 19:10, I was wounded and searching for purpose, and there, God reminded me that His love has the power to restore even the most shattered life.

Restoration Through the Church

The church opened my eyes to a new understanding of family and fellowship, showing me that although I had been broken, I was not beyond repair. In this nurturing environment, I began working through years of buried pain and unresolved emotions, and slowly, I emerged whole again.

The years of dysfunction had fractured me in ways I couldn't fully see. For a long time, I tried to hide behind numbness and self-destructive habits; drinking, smoking, and chasing after meaningless relationships. Then, one day, everything came crashing down, and I felt like a sailor lost at sea with no lifeboat in sight. Yet even then, God's grace reached me.

I discovered that when the Lord Jesus Christ takes hold of a broken life, the story doesn't end in despair, it begins again in redemption.

Rising From the Ashes

Coming into a new relationship with Jesus Christ transformed the person I once was, a broken vessel overflowing with pain, into a soul renewed with passion and purpose.

As 1 John 4:4–6 reminds me, *"greater is He that is in you, than he that is in the world."* God does not see me through the lens of my dysfunction, nor does He measure me by the failures of my family.

I stand where I am today because of His unconditional love, beautifully expressed in John 3:16. Brokenness lasts only for a season, and through God's grace, there is always the promise of rising from the ashes. His love opens the door to healing, growth, and endless possibilities.

I may have been broken, but I was never destroyed, for hope was always there, waiting to be found in the family of God.

Reflection & Renewal

1. How do I respond when faced with difficult truths about my family or myself?
2. What does healthy confrontation look like in my relationships?
3. Am I willing to accept what I cannot change while still working toward peace?
4. In what ways has God used confrontation to heal me rather than harm me?

5. How can I extend grace to others while holding them accountable in love?

Lessons from Chapter Eleven

1. God always has a more excellent plan for your life than you have for yourself.
2. God's love for us is more than the dysfunction we experience.
3. The church is God's place of refuge, where healing can begin.
4. The power of forgiveness can overcome dysfunction.
5. Confronting the problem is difficult, but it works out better than avoiding it.
6. Sometimes people refuse to change, and the only choice is to accept them and move on for your sake.

Chapter Twelve

The Cost of Keeping Up Appearances

When Honesty Makes Others Uncomfortable

People often have a fixed idea of who they think you should be, and the last thing they want is your honesty, especially when that honesty unsettles them. One of the most persistent traits of dysfunction in many Caribbean families is the unspoken rule: *"Don't air your dirty laundry in public."* This mindset has caused generations to suffer in silence, carrying burdens that could have been lifted through truth and openness.

I am fully aware that some parts of this book may make family members uneasy, even angry, but this is my truth. I write not to stir up conflict but to speak from a place of love and conviction. Healing begins where honesty is allowed to breathe, even when it makes us uncomfortable.

The Mask of Appearances

Too many families live behind a façade, pretending all is well while hiding deep pain under the guise of *"keeping up appearances."* The refusal to confront the destruction caused by dysfunctional behaviours has left countless families harvesting the bitter fruit of secrecy and denial.

Society often encourages us to suppress our truths because open conversations expose inherited weaknesses and wounds. But silence is no longer an option. The stakes are too high. No generation can rise above the last if we remain unwilling to face our past and walk courageously in truth.

When the Community Becomes the Judge

Shattering the glasshouse often requires airing the dirty laundry and cleaning the entire house under the watchful eyes of public opinion. Living in a small community has taught me that people often know far more about what happens in our families than they admit. Family issues quickly become community gossip; discussed in bars, taxis, on farms, in the churchyard, and at favourite village hangouts.

Unfortunately, many adults never consider the lasting damage caused when these private matters are repeated in the hearing of children. I remember one morning on my way to school, sitting in a taxi and overhearing a conversation about my mother. I was stunned. What I heard was part of the community's "weekly news bulletin," retold with heavy distortion. For a fifteen-year-old boy, that experience was devastating, leaving scars that words alone could not erase.

Refusing to Play the Game

Overcoming dysfunction requires a firm decision to stop playing the game, because this game can destroy you. We cannot meet everyone's expectations, and it is unrealistic to even try. In this game, deception is the main ingredient, and dysfunctional families have perfected the recipe over generations.

I've come to realize, especially during family gatherings, that things are rarely what they seem. Beneath the laughter and fellowship often lies a deep well of unspoken pain waiting to be addressed, and only honesty can begin the healing process. It's a cruel game where only the strong appear to survive, while in truth, everyone is slowly being wounded.

I am convinced that the devil has targeted the family unit itself, using dysfunction as one of his greatest weapons. Yet we continue to pretend we can handle things privately, when all we are doing is institutionalizing the pain and passing it on to the next generation.

Reflection & Renewal

1. What family "rules of silence" have I accepted without question?
2. How does fear of others' opinions keep me from walking in honesty and freedom?
3. What would it look like to stop "playing the game" and start living authentically?
4. How can I model truth-telling with love in my own family or church community?

5. Am I willing to endure discomfort now for the sake of healing later?

Lessons from Chapter Thirteen

1. Hiding the uncomfortable things about our families allows dysfunction to continue.
2. Truth and reconciliation are part of the healing process.
3. Community gossip fuels the fire of dysfunctional behaviour.
4. The things we try to hide about our families are already public knowledge.
5. When we accept our truth, it makes it difficult for anyone to use it against us.
6. Playing the game has devastating consequences, so don't start playing it. Find ways to address uncomfortable family events.

Chapter Thirteen

Returning to the Root

Returning to the Root

Sometimes moving forward requires going back to the root of the problem. I've had to accept that I need a stable family connection to truly thrive in this world. Things may never be perfect, but I've learned that a flawed family is still better than having none. Each of us moves through the healing process at our own pace, and though the obstacles can feel overwhelming, determination makes progress possible.

Breaking down barriers often means reopening old wounds and allowing ourselves to be vulnerable, a frightening but necessary step. True healing begins when families commit to honest conversations about the past, not in a spirit of blame or condemnation, but with a sincere desire to build something better for those who come after us. It's never easy to unpack years of emotional baggage, but it's the only path to real freedom. Returning to the basics is like spiritual therapy, a cleansing that heals the soul.

Facing the Family Again

Before 1998, I avoided family gatherings because they reminded me too much of my childhood pain. Since becoming a Christian, that has changed. I now see family gatherings as part of my healing process, an opportunity to stay connected to my roots. One of the most valuable lessons I've learned is that running away from problems is not a solution.

Sometimes, at these gatherings, difficult conversations arise. Yet, these uncomfortable moments are necessary to break the dysfunctional cycle. Even though dysfunction may remain, we can still choose whether to live with it consciously or regret never trying to make amends.

Shattering the glasshouse often means confronting your deepest fear. For me, that fear was love and acceptance. Growing up in a dysfunctional family made me suspicious of people's motives. Before 1998, I would withdraw from every gathering, wary of everyone around me. The idea that people could do good without expecting something in return felt foreign.

Over time, I've learned to lower my guard and see the world differently. I realized that people still long for the simple things, love, acceptance, belonging, even in the midst of dysfunction. I had to embrace the truth that my family, imperfect as it is, is still my family. Finding common ground with them, flaws and all, became part of my healing journey.

Letting It Go

The best way to overcome pain is to learn how to let it go. In life, we will all be hurt; sometimes intentionally, sometimes unknowingly. The power to forgive, pick up the pieces, and move forward lies entirely within us. Whether the hurt comes from malice or ignorance, healing is never easy, but if you desire an abundant life, you must dig deep and release it.

Holding on to pain does more harm to us than to the one who caused it. Often, those who hurt us either don't know or don't care about what they've done. Life is complicated, and not every act of pain has an explanation. What matters most is cultivating a resilient spirit, one that forgives and uses pain as a steppingstone toward something extraordinary.

Letting go does not mean accepting bad behaviour or pretending it didn't hurt. It means refusing to let bitterness take root in your heart. One of the devil's most destructive weapons is resentment. If he can keep you bitter, there's no need for him to destroy you, bitterness will do it for him.

When you don't let go, you become a prisoner of your own thoughts, with paranoia and suspicion as constant companions. Letting go means taking a leap of faith into the unknown, trusting that God's peace will meet you there. Most times, the only guarantee you have when you let go is peace of mind, and that's enough.

Misery loves company, and people who cannot release their pain often try to draw others into it. But you have the choice to walk away. Leave the hurt where it belongs, in the past, and move forward into joy and freedom.

Be Bold—Take the First Step

The hardest part of healing family dysfunction is taking the first step. Someone must begin the process of change. In my case, that person was my sister. She was the first to start a family, and her courage to do things differently gave me hope for a better future.

She stepped out in faith and began difficult conversations that led to healing. We can't predict how others will respond but taking that first step is always in our best interest. It may feel painful, like getting a root canal, but it gets easier with time.

That first step begins the long road toward restoration. As one wise saying reminds us, *"The journey of a thousand miles begins with a single step."* I've learned that finding the courage to take that first step often inspires others to do the same. Even those I once thought would never change, eventually followed.

Taking that first step required me to dig deep into my soul, open my heart to forgiveness, and choose hope over hurt. It was worth every bit of the struggle. Holding on to pain keeps us stuck in the past; taking that step is like opening a door and finding yourself surrounded by light.

Yes, the fear of rejection will come. We can't predict how people will respond, but that shouldn't stop us. We must enter every conversation with an open mind and a humble heart, remembering that it's not just about what we want to achieve, but about what must be achieved for the good of everyone involved.

Talk About It.

It's often said that talk is cheap, but the truth is, talk is also *therapeutic.* Families must learn to talk *through* the pain rather than run from it. When we avoid hard conversations, we end up standing at the doorsteps of despair.

Healthy communication is one of the most underused tools for family healing. Too many of us were never taught how to talk things through or resolve conflict peacefully. But talking—honest, respectful talking—can save years of suffering and turn pain into peace.

Emotions can make this difficult. Sometimes, our words become weapons, tearing deeper wounds instead of healing them. It's better to say nothing than to speak words that drag others further into darkness. Words have power, they can destroy, or they can deliver.

Learning to "talk it out" is worth the effort. The conversations that spark healing are rarely comfortable, but they are essential. There can be no meaningful change without them. Someone must be bold enough to start that talk, no matter how awkward or painful it feels at first. Once you begin, the conversation becomes a bridge toward hope and healing, and before long, you'll find yourself cruising down the highway of restoration.

Reflection & Renewal

1. What "roots" in my past still need to be confronted for true healing to begin?
2. What does letting go mean to me, and what am I still holding on to?

3. Who might God be calling me to take the first step toward reconciliation with?

4. How can I turn painful conversations into opportunities for healing?

5. What role does honesty play in creating a healthy, loving family environment?

Lessons from Chapter Thirteen

1. We must speak the truth, even when it makes us uncomfortable. Writing about dysfunction is not about getting back at anyone; it is to initiate the healing process.

2. Covering up dysfunctional behaviour is a game of deception that the devil wants us to play. Playing this game has devastating consequences.

3. Dealing with dysfunctional behaviour requires going back to the problem's root cause.

4. Getting to the root cause will demand that we confront our deepest fears.

5. Sometimes the people we love the most are the ones that seem to cause us the most pain.

6. Somebody must be courageous enough to take the first step to deal with dysfunctional behaviour.

7. Learning how to have healthy conversations about dysfunctional behaviour helps in the healing process.

Chapter Fourteen

Shattering the Glasshouse: The Family Factor

You Are Not Alone

The journey to finding purpose and living in abundance begins when you accept that you are not alone in your struggles. While writing this book, I discovered that my family's issues were not unique. Many others are living with the aftermath of dysfunction, holding on to hope that healing is still possible.

Through my research and countless conversations, I became convinced that all is not lost. In every family, there are individuals willing to do what it takes to shatter the glasshouse. My greatest lesson from this experience is that breaking dysfunction requires teamwork. The family that learns to stand together will be victorious and secure its future against the destructive cycles of the past.

A Shift in Mindset

If we can change the way families think, the damage done by years of dysfunctional behaviour can be repaired. I had to undergo a transformation of my own thought process, and it was neither quick nor easy. Yet the reward was worth every ounce of effort.

The greatest obstacle to overcoming dysfunction is a mind that refuses to change. Once we understand how deeply our actions affect future generations, we realize that we cannot afford to remain the same. *Shattering the glasshouse* demands a new approach, a willingness to confront the patterns that have kept families bound for too long.

If we fail to do this, future generations will inherit the same mistakes we made, trapped in the same painful cycles. The cost of inaction is far too high.

The Meaning of Family

The family is the foundation of everything that exists. Without it remaining healthy, we are like sheep without a shepherd. When the family is fractured, every other part of society suffers. But when it thrives, it produces strong individuals, healthy communities, and stable nations.

To explain what the family represents—and what it should mean—I want to use the acronym **FAMILY** as both a mirror and a guide. Each letter represents two contrasting realities: the negative aspects of dysfunction and the positive traits that bring restoration.

Chapter Fourteen
(continued)

The Two Sides of FAMILY

The Positive FAMILY

- Fun
- Appreciation
- Memories
- Irreplaceable
- Love
- Yielding

Fun

A key feature of any healthy family is the ability to have fun. By fun, I mean engaging in activities that are amusing, joyful, and light-hearted, moments that build belonging and friendship. Families that laugh and play together seem to handle life's challenges more effectively. When we let go of our inhibitions and embrace wholesome enjoyment, the results can be deeply therapeutic.

I have written before about my love for family gatherings; one of the reasons is that they allow me to have fun. It took time for us to get there, but it was worth every step. Families that learn to have fun together begin to heal. When families play, children grow in confidence, relationships strengthen, and good memories replace the pain of dysfunction. There is nothing quite like quality time spent recapturing what was lost.

Appreciation

Expressions of gratitude, admiration, and acknowledgment are essential for a healthy family. Every person needs to know that they belong and are valued. A lack of appreciation is a sure sign of dysfunction, often creating emotional distance and resentment.

Appreciation helps to neutralize toxic emotions that arise from past hurts. When we begin to look at each other without suspicion or bitterness, and instead with genuine gratitude, we create room for healing. Seeing one another through the eyes of Christ changes how we relate. Every family member has a role to play in fostering growth and stability. When appreciation becomes the family's language, problems become easier to solve, even those rooted in dysfunction.

Memories

One of the family's sacred responsibilities is creating lasting memories. The problem is not making memories, it's making good ones. Dysfunction often fills our minds with painful recollections we wish we could forget. But that was never God's design.

God intended families to be the gatekeepers of what is sacred—and memories are among His greatest gifts. To heal, we must start creating moments worth remembering. Good memories preserve hope and strengthen identity. Since deciding to shatter the glasshouse, I've found that joyful memories now stand out more clearly than the painful ones. We may not always create perfect moments, but when relationships are healthy, the good memories multiply.

Irreplaceable

The word *irreplaceable* means impossible to substitute, and that's what families are. We don't get to choose the family we are born into; we learn to love the one we have. There is no such thing as a perfect family, each has its own challenges.

The temptation to distance ourselves from those who cause the most conflict is real. But even difficult relatives serve a purpose. A major step toward breaking dysfunction is learning to love people as they are, without excusing their behaviour. Many act only out of the knowledge they possess, and growth takes time.

Our families, despite their flaws, are irreplaceable. More often than not, they are the ones who come to our rescue in times of need. Loving them despite shortcomings is one of the greatest tests of maturity.

Love

There is more to life than all the treasures in the world. A family rooted in love can overcome almost anything. This love is not based on convenience or emotion; it's a deep commitment to work through difficulty and stay united through faith.

Love is the ultimate weapon against dysfunction. As 1 Peter 4:8 reminds us, *"Love covers a multitude of sins."* When families choose love over resentment, they bring the spinning wheel of dysfunction to a stop. Love pushes us beyond comfort zones and helps us rediscover our humanity. Families that learn to love will always find their way back to wholeness.

Yielding

Though the word *yielding* often carries a negative tone—implying surrender or weakness, it can be profoundly positive. Sometimes, to gain more, we must give up something. Healthy families understand that compromise is not defeat but wisdom.

Yielding means surrendering pride, listening with empathy, and prioritizing peace over power. Dysfunctional families often fail to do this, remaining rigid and resistant to change. But flexibility fosters understanding. By yielding in love, families strengthen rather than lose themselves.

The Negative FAMILY

- Failing
- Anger
- Messy
- Insecure
- Lacking
- Yammering

Failing
Without intervention, dysfunctional families become failing families, stuck in cycles of silence and denial. Many do not recognize how their actions damage the next generation. They prefer maintaining appearances to facing hard truths. But pretending all is well never brings healing.

To stop failing, families must be honest. We must lay our cards on the table and commit to dealing with what's broken. Shattering the glasshouse begins with courageous transparency.

Anger
Dysfunctional families are often filled with deep resentment. This anger, built over generations, simmers until it explodes, sometimes into violence. It poisons relationships and destroys trust.

Unresolved anger never heals; it only hardens hearts. It must be named, confronted, and released. Hidden anger is destructive; it shatters the glasshouse but never rebuilds it.

Insecure

In dysfunctional families, insecurity breeds suspicion. People question motives, compete for affection, and operate out of fear. Even those closest to the "inner circle" worry about losing favour.

This insecurity keeps the family on the edge, waiting for collapse. True security only comes when love and acceptance replace comparison and fear.

Lacking

A dysfunctional family lacks insight, honesty, and the will to change. They struggle to communicate feelings and avoid conflict, allowing tension to fester into generational feuds.

Often, members who dream of a better future are scorned or ostracized. But progress requires courage. The family will continue to lack healing until it chooses growth over comfort.

Yammering

I chose *yammering*, meaning to complain endlessly because it captures a destructive pattern in many families. Chronic complaining drains energy, breeds negativity, and blocks progress.

Some people can find a problem in every solution. Until families take responsibility for their actions, dysfunction will persist. Healing begins when we stop blaming and start building.

Reflection & Renewal

1. Which version of FAMILY best represents my family today, positive or negative?
2. Which of the six traits (Fun, Appreciation, Memories, Irreplaceable, Love, Yielding) do we need to cultivate most?
3. What steps can we take this month to start building good memories and showing appreciation?
4. Am I contributing to healing or to dysfunction in my family?
5. How can I model the love and yielding spirit that leads to transformation?

Chapter Fifteen

Restoring What's Broken

The Importance of Repairing Broken Bonds

Repairing family relationships in dysfunctional households is essential to the well-being and harmony of everyone involved. When family dynamics are unhealthy, the emotional and mental impact can last for generations. Addressing these issues is critical for emotional healing, stability, and growth.

Rebuilding relationships doesn't just strengthen the family unit; it equips members with better communication and conflict resolution skills. Healing the home environment breaks the cycle of dysfunction, setting a new example for future generations. It provides closure, restores trust, and cultivates belonging, all of which enrich the lives of every family member.

Restoring family relationships also shapes how individuals interact outside the home. Those who address and overcome family wounds often become more empathetic, emotionally balanced, and resilient. The ripple effect of reconciliation extends beyond the family, influencing friendships, workplaces, and entire communities. Healthy homes build healthy societies.

For the Love of My Father

Repairing my relationship with my father has had one of the most profound impacts on my life. I would not be who I am today without the stability and renewed bond that now exists between us. Life has a way of teaching us lessons, often the hard way.

If someone had told me twenty years ago that my dad and I would have had such a strong relationship, I would have laughed in disbelief. During my teenage years, our relationship was turbulent. I resented his choices, confused by what seemed to be his willingness to throw away much to gain so little. For years, I avoided him completely, unaware that while I was building a wall of resentment, he was quietly fighting his own demons.

At one point, I convinced myself I didn't need him to survive. As the oldest child, I saw and understood more than my siblings. I witnessed my mother's pain and silence in the face of his womanizing. I remember his excuses, his promises to do better, and his contradictions, an angel one moment and the devil's messenger the next. He was a man torn between knowing the right thing and doing the wrong one.

Today, I refer to him in the past tense not because he's gone, but because he's changed. A few years before he left for England, something shifted in him. I began to see my father differently, and that change altered my understanding of him.

For anyone struggling with a strained relationship with a parent, I encourage you to explore their story. Learn their history before you draw your conclusions. I had to step out from behind the wall of resentment and intentionally rediscover the man I called "Dad." What I found transformed my heart. I learned that shattering the glasshouse requires compassion, and that means confronting not only our own pain but also the hidden battles our parents have fought for generations.

Healing the Ties That Bind

There is a saying that "children live what they learn." I would add: *fathers live what they learn too.* Show me a father who has failed, and I will show you generations of men shaped by dysfunction. While my father bears responsibility for his actions, his story is inseparable from the legacy he inherited.

When generational dysfunction goes unaddressed, it sets the next generation up for failure in parenting, relationships, and identity. My father's struggles were part of a larger pattern, one that stretched back through my grandfather and even further. My grandfather was a womanizer, just like his father before him. Without realizing it, I began walking down the same path until I decided that something had to change.

What's more, this same flawed attitude toward women existed in both my paternal and maternal family lines. My brother and I inherited a double portion of dysfunction, but also the opportunity to break the chain. I have seen firsthand that unless there is intentional intervention, we unconsciously repeat what we've lived.

In recent years, my father has made deliberate efforts to be a better man. He now expresses love to his grandchildren, takes interest in our plans, and has even begun organizing his affairs for the future. He may not always say "I love you" aloud, but his actions speak volumes. His growth is proof that it's never too late to heal. Consistent effort can indeed shatter the glasshouse.

Dear Dad…

Dear Dad,

It's strange how they say time heals because I never imagined I would write you this letter. Growing up, we were far from close. You made choices I could not understand, and they often left me confused and hurt. It broke my heart to see Mom cry and to feel like you didn't care. You were gone when I needed you most, and so I learned to live without you. For years, I believed you would never change.

But now I see things differently. While I was wrestling with pain, you were battling your own demons. I didn't know the hardships you faced — growing up in the country, feeling neglected, losing your mother so young, and carrying the weight of unrealized dreams. I didn't know how much fear and disappointment shaped your life. Now, I understand. I still hold you accountable for your past, but I forgive you, Dad.

I see how hard you've tried to make up for lost time, and I want you to know that it matters. You've been judged by your past, but your present shows growth, humility, and heart. You've kept dreaming, even after setbacks. You've never pretended to be perfect, and I respect that.

Dad, you are a work in progress — and that's okay. Sometimes you get it right, sometimes you don't, but you never stop trying. I am proud to be your son. The lessons I've learned from your failures and your faith have shaped the man I've become. As I raise my own children, I understand the sacrifices of fatherhood in a new way.

Thank you for not giving up — not on life, not on yourself, and not on us. The world may never applaud you, but I do. I love you, and I am grateful that you are my father.

Your son,

Paul A. Blake

Reflection & Renewal

1. What steps can I take today to repair a broken family relationship?
2. What barriers, emotional, mental, or spiritual, keep me from forgiveness?
3. How has my family history shaped my current relationships?
4. What can I learn from the struggles of my parents or guardians?
5. Who in my family needs to hear "I forgive you" or "I understand"?

Lessons from Chapter Fifteen

1. A father is an important element in a young man's life as he transitions to adulthood.
2. We are not our fathers. We don't have to live our lives making the same mistakes they did.
3. Any relationship can be repaired if there is a willingness to forgive without conditions.
4. If we allow people to grow, they will surprise us. Judge people by their past mistakes.
5. Make use of the opportunity to say what is on your heart. The result may bring you joy.

Chapter Sixteen

Reclaiming the Sacred Call of Fatherhood

A Call to Rise

After repairing my relationship with my father, I began to see the deeper crisis facing our families, it wasn't just my story, but the story of a generation. The absence of fathers has left a void that no mother, no matter how strong, can fully fill. This gap has created generations of confused, hurting, and misguided sons and daughters.

The theme for Jamaica's Parent's Month 2020, *"Fathers Arise! Lead and Be Wise,"* could not have been more prophetic. It captures what our society desperately needs today, men who will stand up, take responsibility, and reclaim their God-given role as leaders of their homes and protectors of their families. The truth is, the glasshouse can never truly be shattered until fathers return to their posts.

All around us, we see the consequences of their absence, broken homes, directionless boys, and weary mothers struggling to fill a gap they were never meant to bear alone. Something is brewing beneath the surface of our communities, and if we fail to address it, the results will be devastating. Fathers must arise, not in pride or power, but in humility, courage, and wisdom.

Standing in the Gap

Fatherhood is both a gift and a responsibility. It is one of the most sacred trusts God gives to a man. Yet, too many men have abdicated that role, leaving children to navigate life without the steadying hand of a father's guidance.

We must remember that it's not how we start that matters, it's how we finish. Many fathers have stumbled, but falling does not mean failure. Redemption begins the moment a man decides to stand again. The same God who redeems broken lives can restore broken fathers.

Every father has the capacity to shape destiny. The words we speak, the choices we make, and the example we set are seeds that grow in the hearts of our children. When we are absent, physically, emotionally, or spiritually, those seeds never mature, and weeds of dysfunction grow instead.

It's time for men to stand in the gap for their families. Rise up, not because it's easy, but because the next generation depends on it.

Fathers Who Lead

Leadership is not dominant, it is service. A father's authority is not meant to oppress but to protect. God has entrusted men with the responsibility to lead their families in love, wisdom, and faith.

When men stop leading, the family loses direction. Our homes, schools, and communities reveal this truth every day. The prisons are filled with young men whose fathers were absent or disengaged. The statistics may be grim, but the stories behind them are even more painful. Each represents a child who needed a father's presence but instead met his silence.

Leadership in the home is not about being in charge, it's about being responsible. A wise father listens, nurtures, and corrects with love. He leads not by command but by example. Sons learn how to treat women by watching their fathers. Daughters learn what love looks like by observing how their fathers treat their mothers.

We cannot compete with women for the right to lead. God designed the family as a partnership, each role vital, each voice necessary. But when men abdicate leadership, women are left to bear the weight of responsibility alone. This is not about who is more capable; it's about divine order and spiritual balance.

Our sons must see leadership modeled before they are expected to lead. They must see humility in their fathers before they can understand strength. Leadership that begins at home will echo through generations.

Wise Fathers Build, Foolish Fathers Break

A wise father is not one who never fails but one who learns from his failures. Every decision a father makes carries the weight of legacy. Foolishness destroys what wisdom patiently builds.

Many fathers have inherited the patterns of dysfunction from their own fathers, and without divine intervention, those patterns will continue. Wisdom begins with awareness, the willingness to see that what has always been done is not always right. The Bible reminds us, "Wisdom is the principal thing; therefore, get wisdom" (Proverbs 4:7).

To be wise fathers, we must seek God's guidance daily. Wisdom does not come by accident; it comes by intention; by prayer, reflection, and surrender. The wise father understands that every word spoken in anger, every promise broken, and every moment of neglect plants something in a child's soul.

Wise fathers are not perfect men; they are humble men. They understand that leadership is stewardship and that their families belong first to God. Their role is to protect, nurture, and guide those entrusted to them. When a father leads with wisdom, the family becomes a sanctuary of peace and stability.

When a man lacks wisdom, he becomes the architect of his own destruction. He tears down his home with his own hands through carelessness and pride. But when wisdom rules, the home becomes what God intended, a haven of grace, love, and unity.

The Legacy of a Father

A father's influence never ends; it echoes across generations. God has entrusted fathers with His most sacred treasure—the family. He expects us to return it to Him better than we received it.

The family is not ours to control; it is ours to cultivate. Every father must ask: *Am I leaving a legacy of faith or a trail of brokenness?* The answer will determine whether the next generation inherits healing or continues the cycle of pain.

Fathers, arise. Your time is now. Be the voice your children can trust, the rock your family can lean on, and the example your sons and daughters can follow. The world may not applaud your efforts, but

Heaven will. The glasshouse can and must be shattered—but only if fathers rise, lead, and walk wisely.

Reflection Questions

1. In what ways have I reflected the fatherhood of God in my home?
2. What past mistakes do I need to acknowledge and learn from?
3. How can I model servant leadership to my children today?
4. What one area of my life requires wisdom before I can lead well?
5. What will my legacy as a father look like if I continue on my current path?

Lessons from Chapter Sixteen

1. Every child needs a father or father figure in his/her life. Where male role models are lacking, the growth and development of children are at a disadvantage.
2. Sometimes forgiveness is the only option to repair a damaged relationship with our fathers.
3. If you can't have a conversation with your father, an open letter to him is an excellent place to start.
4. What kind of father do you want to be for your child(ren)?
5. If you did not have a father in your life, would you be willing to help mentor young men?

Chapter Seventeen

From Shattered Walls to Strong Foundations

The Glasshouse and the Family

The glasshouse is a metaphor for dysfunctional families. Breaking down destructive patterns is critical for the survival of our homes, not tomorrow, but now. We cannot delay the work of healing until the next generation. While we must shatter the glasshouse, we must also ensure the foundation remains firm. We cannot become so focused on breaking generational curses that we forget we are dealing with real people, real pain, and real souls.

When the glasshouse finally shatters, those who remain must find healing to rebuild their purpose. God never designed families to live within fragile walls of fear, secrecy, and dysfunction. His will is that our homes reflect His image, places of peace, love, and nurture.

Yet today, the family is under threat. All around us, we see homes crumbling under pressure; domestic violence, neglected children, crumbling marriages, and communities torn apart by hopelessness. Our societies are broken because our families are broken. Too often, we pour our resources into treating the symptoms, crime, education gaps, divorce, while ignoring the disease at the root: the collapse of the family.

For generations, we have been building glasshouses, and now the cracks are showing. The family cries out from within those walls, yearning to breathe again.

Breaking the Glass

The glasshouse spans generations: it does not discriminate between rich or poor, educated or uneducated. Its walls are reinforced by silence, shame, and fear. Many know their homes are collapsing, but pride keeps them pretending that "all is well."

Breaking the glass begins with courage, the courage of one person, one voice, or one family member willing to say, *"This stops with me."* We may not have chosen to be born into dysfunction but remaining there is a choice. Too often, we have become so comfortable in chaos that we mistake it for normalcy. Dysfunction may have shaped our history, but it does not have to determine our destiny.

Glasshouses were never meant for human habitation. They are temporary structures, beautiful from afar but dangerous to live in. It's time to move out, to build homes that are solid, healthy, and whole.

Breaking the glass requires reshaping how we think about family. Families are not burdens to manage; they are the bedrock of civilization. The glasshouse has stood for too long because we keep patching the cracks instead of uprooting the foundation. We deal with the symptoms while ignoring the sickness. Until we are ready to confront the uncomfortable truths; the lies, the abuse, the pride, the neglect, we will never heal.

Breaking the glass means laying everything bare, letting light expose what has been hidden. Like the walls of Jericho, these barriers will only fall when we face them together, with honesty, prayer, and unity of heart.

Build Homes, Not Mansions

Once the glass is shattered, the real work begins, rebuilding. But what are we building toward? In a world obsessed with status and wealth, we must resist the urge to build mansions while our homes remain broken.

We need to return to building homes, not houses of luxury, but havens of love. Dysfunction thrives where appearances matter more than relationships. A home does not have to be grand; it must be grounded.

The home is the oldest and most sacred human institution. Across every culture, it carries the same essence, belonging, safety, and love. When our homes are broken, our societies crumble. Broken homes create broken people; broken people build broken communities. The cycle spins until someone decides to repair it.

God designed the home as sacred ground, a training ground for character and compassion. Parenting is not a job we can afford to fail. We must create environments where children are valued and secure, where mothers and fathers cooperate to raise emotionally healthy and spiritually grounded individuals.

Healing begins when we stop masking our pain and start confronting it. We cannot heal families while clinging to the very patterns that broke them. Healing begins when we say, *"This ends with me."*

Care for Your Own Family

Peter Tosh once sang, *"If you live in a glass house, don't throw stones."* His words echo through generations, a reminder that hypocrisy has no place in healing.

We live in a culture where it's easier to fix others than to face ourselves. From church pews to boardrooms, everyone has an opinion about someone else's dysfunction, but few have the courage to address their own. Before we can fix the world, we must fix our homes.

Shattering the glasshouse begins with one family at a time, starting with your own. Before we critique others, we must confront our own patterns of neglect, secrecy, and avoidance. The journey begins with honesty.

Writing this book has been part of my healing. I could not speak about transformation without first facing the truth about my own life. No degree or training could have prepared me for the day I had to look in the mirror and admit, *"I need help."* Dysfunction is not a curse, it's a challenge. It's an opportunity to grow, to unlearn, and to rebuild.

Our families are our most valuable assets. When the family is healthy, the nation thrives. But when the family is fractured, no system can stand in its place. We must invest in our own homes before attempting to repair others.

We cannot afford to be experts in everyone else's life while neglecting our own. Each of us must take responsibility for the health of our family unit. If we ignore our homes, the glasshouse will only grow stronger, and the cycle of pain will continue.

Understanding our family's history is the key to breaking the cycle. Every family carries its own struggles, but awareness brings power. We cannot heal what we refuse to name. By confronting our history, we reclaim our future.

Reflection and Renewal

1. What "glass walls" still stand in your family that need to be broken?
2. How can you begin rebuilding your home with love and honesty?
3. Which patterns from your family history do you need to unlearn?
4. What role can faith and forgiveness play in rebuilding your family's foundation?
5. What will your legacy be — another glasshouse or a home that stands firm?

Lessons from Chapter Seventeen

1. We cannot separate generational dysfunction from the people we are trying to help.
2. To overcome dysfunctional behaviours we must place greater focus on building healthy families.
3. Building better families requires a hands-on approach from all stakeholders. It is not the responsibility of a selected few.
4. Before we look outward, we must look inward and address our own family dysfunctions.
5. We are not healing our families for just the present; we are seeking to affect future generations.
6. Healthy families are the building blocks of successful nations.

Chapter Eighteen

Self-Care to Overcome Brokenness

Healing Yourself to Heal the Family

The Weight of Dysfunction

One of the most noticeable habits of people who come from dysfunctional families is their tendency to attract others who share similar brokenness. Like magnets, pain recognizes pain. Many who grow up in dysfunctional homes struggle to love themselves, opening their lives to unfulfilling and even harmful relationships.

The craving to feel loved and accepted often leads us into the arms of people who trample our emotions. We give, we pour out, we overextend, only to find ourselves drained and disappointed. Broken people struggle to set boundaries, and where there are no boundaries, there can be no peace.

Instead of nurturing ourselves, we chase the love of others who cannot give what they do not have. We end up wasting energy trying to fix what was never ours to fix. But healing begins when we stop running after what broke us and start turning inward, to care for the soul that God designed for purpose.

Recognizing the Patterns

As I've grown older, I've had to face hard truths about the people I once allowed into my life. Many of them were draining my energy, not replenishing it. I sought their approval and received pain in return. I wanted to belong so badly that I ignored the cost.

Looking back, I realize I gave away the best parts of myself, hoping to earn love I never received. I expected others to fix me when I should have been learning to love myself. The lies I told myself became the truth I lived by: *"I am not enough."*

But the truth is, I was created in God's image. I was enough from the beginning. Dysfunction had convinced me otherwise, but grace has been teaching me to see differently.

The First Step: Caring for the Self

Many of us struggle with guilt when we start focusing on self-care. We believe we are selfish when, in reality, we are simply learning to survive. Self-care is not self-centered, it is soul-centered.

When I finally began taking care of myself, I realized that I had spent years living for everyone else. I thought I owed explanations to the world. I refused to break free from the emotional shackles that kept me bound to approval and people-pleasing.

I'm not alone. Countless others are trapped in the same cycle; spinning, striving, and surviving, without ever truly living. But we cannot heal our families or fix our relationships without first addressing our own mental and emotional health. Healing begins with the mind.

Anyone who has broken free from dysfunction has started by renewing their thinking. *"Be transformed by the renewing of your mind,"* says Romans 12:2. Healing begins not in the hands, but in the head, in the space where we choose truth over lies, growth over guilt, and peace over pain. Self-care is not optional. It is a divine responsibility.

Broken People Don't Heal Broken People

One of the biggest lies we tell ourselves is that broken people can fix other broken people. While two people who share pain can find comfort in understanding, true healing requires more than shared suffering, it requires wholeness.

I've seen it in my own family: instead of seeking help, we convinced ourselves we could fix each other. We passed our pain around like an heirloom, carrying wounds from one generation to the next. The result was predictable: surface healing without real transformation.

You cannot pour from an empty cup. You cannot give what you do not possess. Self-care is not a luxury; it is a necessity if you are to be of any value to those around you.

To care for others, you must first be cared for. To carry someone else's burden, you must first strengthen your own shoulders. As Jesus said, *"Love your neighbor as yourself."* Notice, He did not say "instead of." The command assumes that you first know how to love yourself in a godly, healthy way.

Returning to the Place of Hurt

One of the tragedies of brokenness is that we often return to the very places that wounded us. We go back, not because they are safe, but because they are familiar. Familiar pain feels less frightening than unfamiliar peace.

The illusion of control keeps us stuck. We tell ourselves that because we function well enough; working, raising children, serving in church, we must be healed. But functioning is not the same as flourishing. We can be high-performing and deeply broken at the same time.

When we continually return to our places of hurt, whether it's a toxic family dynamic, an unhealthy relationship, or a self-destructive mindset, we are building altars to our pain. The mountain of dysfunction looms large, and we camp at its base, afraid to climb higher or walk away.

But that mountain will eventually crumble. And when it does, it will take everything standing beneath it.

Breaking Free from the Place of Pain

The greatest obstacle to abundant living is the inability to let go of the people and places that hurt us. Parents, spouses, friends, some have held our hearts hostage for years, and we keep returning to them, hoping for closure they cannot provide.

Healing requires separation, not from love, but from bondage. We cannot heal in the same environment that broke us. We must, in love and wisdom, create distance from the patterns and people that perpetuate our pain.

Breaking free does not mean burning bridges; it means learning when to cross them and when to stop rebuilding what God has called us to release. Fear of the unknown keeps many trapped, but freedom often lies on the other side of fear.

You cannot discover what's next if you keep running back to what was. God cannot fill your hands with new blessings while they are still clutching the past.

So, take a deep breath. Let go. Trust that God has better waiting for you beyond the glass walls of pain.

A Renewed Mind for a Restored Life

Healing is not a one-time event; it's a daily decision. Every morning, you choose whether to live as a victim of your past or a steward of your healing.

To overcome brokenness, we must:

- **Acknowledge our pain.** Denial delays deliverance.
- **Seek help.** Therapy, prayer, and community are not signs of weakness but steps toward wholeness.
- **Forgive ourselves and others.** Forgiveness is the bridge to freedom.
- **Establish boundaries.** They protect peace and honor self-worth.
- **Rest in God's love.** His grace restores what brokenness destroys.

Brokenness is not your identity, it's an experience. You are not the wound; you are the one God is healing.

Reflection Questions

1. What areas of your life still need healing from family dysfunction?
2. In what ways have you neglected self-care out of guilt or fear?
3. Are there relationships you need to release in order to heal?
4. What does loving yourself through God's eyes look like today?
5. How can you begin building a lifestyle that nurtures emotional and spiritual health?

Lessons from Chapter Eighteen

1. Broken people tend to attract other broken people. If dysfunction goes unchecked, the results can be devastating.
2. Broken people need to be healed before they can form healthy relationships.
3. Without self-care, we are prone to repeating past mistakes.
4. Self-care is not selfish. Taking care of ourselves puts us in a better position to take care of others.
5. Healing from brokenness will require us to confront our fears and the things that make us uncomfortable.
6. Returning to the scene of the place of hurt does little to aid in the healing process.

Chapter Nineteen

How a Broken Vessel Wins God's Favour

When God Turns Wounds into Worship

From Brokenness to Breakthrough

As I write this chapter, I am reminded of a season in my life that few know about, a time that tested the very foundation of my faith. Joseph's declaration to his brothers in Genesis 50:19–20 echoes through my story:

"Don't be afraid of me. Am I in the place of God? You intended to harm me, but God intended it for good."

Like Joseph, I have learned that even the glasshouses others build to confine us will shatter when God's hand moves. The very things meant to destroy us often become the instruments God uses to shape our destiny.

In 1998, when I stepped out of a world of brokenness and into the arms of Christ, I thought my season of struggle had ended. But another storm was waiting, a storm that would strip away pride, break my spirit, and teach me to trust God in ways I never imagined.

The Power of Words

I've often written about the power of words, how they shape our thinking, fuel our fears, and even dictate our destiny. Words can build or break, heal or harm.

I vividly remember the words of two individuals who almost pushed me into a pit of self-destruction. These memories bring pain even now, but I have found healing in sharing them, believing that my story may light the way for someone else's deliverance.

The church, though a refuge, is not free from wounded people who wound others. My intention is not to criticize, but to remind us that even within the body of Christ, brokenness can manifest in harmful ways when left unhealed.

Wounded in the House of Friends

One Sunday afternoon, as I prepared to leave my hometown for Bible school, a sister in the congregation whispered words that cut deep into my heart:

"I hope you have no intention of coming back here to preach, because nobody wants you here."

Those words branded my soul. They followed me into classrooms, prayers, and sleepless nights. For years, I lived in fear of rejection, hiding my talents and minimizing my potential. But God, in His mercy, began to dismantle the lies I had accepted as truth.

I learned that someone else's opinion of me does not define me, it defines them. Their words could not cancel God's purpose. What they meant for harm, God was already using for my good.

The Second Blow

My second encounter with pain came when I dared to ask the church for financial help to pursue my studies. That day, I swallowed my pride and made my request publicly. What happened next nearly shattered my spirit.

The brother in charge of finance stood up, threw his checkbook to the ground, and said with cold disdain:

"If I am the one to write a check for you to attend school, it will not happen."

I was crushed. Humiliated. Tears streamed down my face as I stood there, speechless. But even in that moment of rejection, God was preparing a greater revelation: that no man's refusal can stop a door God intends to open.

When God Writes the Last Word

Despite the rejection, God sustained me. I survived four years of study without institutional support, sustained by grace and the kindness of believers who embodied true Christian love.

By 2002, I was enrolled at the University of the West Indies while still attending the Jamaica School of Preaching. Those were grueling years—financially, emotionally, spiritually. But each challenge became a classroom in God's school of endurance.

When I finally graduated—debt-free, with honours from both institutions, I knew I had witnessed a miracle. Miss Joan's son, once dismissed as a failure, walked across the stage as a vessel refined by fire.

The same community that whispered "He will never make it" now watched as God turned their words into fuel for my calling. What once felt like shame had become a testimony.

Lessons from the Glasshouse

People often construct glasshouses around our lives to keep us contained. Whether intentional or not, their words and judgments can trap us in cycles of fear and self-doubt.

For months after those painful moments, I lived under the weight of their words. I behaved like the *"nothing"* they said I was. But grace has a way of rewriting the story. God began teaching me that freedom comes not from erasing the past, but from reclaiming it through faith.

My passion for counselling and psychology grew out of those experiences. Studying human behaviour helped me understand why hurt people hurt others, and why I had allowed their opinions to shape me. I learned that healing is not about forgetting what was said, it's about refusing to let it control who you become.

God's Favour on Broken Vessels

If there's one truth, I want every reader to carry, it's this: **God delights in using broken vessels.**

He does not discard the cracked pot; He fills it with grace so His glory can shine through the fractures. The very areas of weakness become the channels of His strength. The rejection that once crushed us becomes the testimony that lifts others.

Romans 8:28 is not a cliché—it is a lifeline:

"And we know that in all things God works for the good of those who love Him, who have been called according to His purpose."

Those who wounded me were not my enemies—they were instruments in God's hands. Their actions tested my faith but strengthened my resolve. Today, I can look back and thank God for every painful word, every closed door, and every lonely night.

A New Identity in Christ

I now understand that not everyone will see you through the eyes of grace. Some will only remember your failures; others will never forgive your progress. But that's not your burden to carry.

We are not defined by what people think, but by who God says we are. Their disbelief does not diminish our destiny. If they could see what God is doing behind the scenes, they would have to revise their judgment.

I am no longer the wounded boy seeking approval, I am a redeemed man walking in purpose. My pain became my preparation, my rejection became my redirection, and my story became a sermon of grace.

Reflections: The Victory of a Broken Vessel

1. **Rejection is redirection.** What others meant for harm, God uses for your promotion.
2. **Pain produces purpose.** The places that broke you are the very places God will use you.
3. **Your worth is not up for debate.** It was settled at the cross.
4. **Favour follows faithfulness.** Even in your lowest valley, God's favour will find you.
5. **You are a vessel, not a victim.** The cracks in your life are the openings through which God's light shines.

Lessons from Chapter Twenty

1. God can use our broken, dysfunctional lives for our benefit and His glory.
2. The church, though a place of refuge, has people with flaws who don't always behave like Christ.
3. People will try to destroy you, but time will teach you that you are stronger than you thought.
4. There are more people on your side cheering for you than those who would want to see you fail.
5. The best revenge you can have is to prove those who would destroy you wrong. Don't get bitter; get better.
6. The taste of victory is sweet; never give up, even when the deck is stacked against you.

Chapter Twenty

Breaking the Silence on Sex and Shame

We Don't About That Stuff

The Silent Demon in the Family

Among the most persistent taboos in dysfunctional families is the uncomfortable silence surrounding sex and sexuality. The subject is treated as forbidden, shameful, and dangerous, only surfacing in moments of scandal or crisis. In many homes, sex is seen as a disgusting or sinful act, even within marriage. Conversations about its beauty, purpose, or boundaries are practically non-existent.

This silence has created a culture of confusion and fear. For many, sex was demonized, while those who secretly abused others used that silence as a cloak to hide their sin. In our effort to guard the so-called *"sex demon,"* we opened the door to deeper wounds, abuse, secrecy, and shame that still haunt families today.

Growing Up in Silence

Even as I write, this subject makes me uncomfortable. Despite years of speaking publicly on issues of sex and relationships, I still find it difficult to discuss it in a family context. Like many others, I never had a real conversation about sex with my parents or grandparents.

When I was a child, sex was a *dirty word.* No one talked about where babies came from, menstruation, wet dreams, or the changes that come with adolescence. If you dared to ask, you'd be met with fury or silence. "Big people ting" was the only explanation you got, and that was supposed to be enough.

But it wasn't just my family. Across our communities, this silence was widespread. The sexually liberated were ridiculed and branded with shame, while unmarried pregnant women carried public disgrace. Boys who followed the examples of their unfaithful fathers were labelled *"wutless."* Each of these responses added to the confusion and pain surrounding something God created as beautiful and sacred.

Guarding the Demon

The so-called "sex demon" had to be guarded at all costs. The older generation feared that if the topic were ever discussed openly, young people would lose all moral restraint. But that fear produced the very chaos it tried to prevent.

Because no one taught us, many of us learned about sex from the wrong sources, the community gossip, peers who were equally uninformed, or pornography that distorted our understanding. Others suffered through unwanted sexual experiences or abuse, carrying scars that lingered for decades.

All of this could have been prevented if families had been willing to replace secrecy with truth and fear with guidance.

Undressing the Demon: Let's Talk About It

Refusing to talk about sex does not protect our families, it damages them. It's time we strip away the shame and start having healthy, honest, age-appropriate discussions. Sex is not demonic, dirty, or unholy. It is a divine gift that must be handled with wisdom and respect.

Here are a few lies we must confront:

1. "Sex is dirty and shameful."
This is one of the most damaging myths passed down through generations. Society's over-sexualization has twisted the conversation, making us retreat even further into silence. But sex, within God's design, is pure, beautiful, and meant for connection.

We must teach our children that sexual feelings are natural, not evil. Let's stop using shame as a tool for control. The only thing dirty about sex is the ignorance we continue to pass down.

2. "Sex is dangerous."
Many children are told that sex is dangerous and must be avoided at all costs. While it's true that sexual activity outside God's boundaries can have serious consequences, the act itself is not dangerous, it's divine when understood correctly.

Parents must create safe spaces for age-appropriate discussions. Talking about sex will not make children reckless; it will make them responsible. Silence, on the other hand, breeds secrecy and rebellion.

3. "Girls must be pure; boys will be boys."
Dysfunction often punishes women while excusing men. Girls are taught fear, while boys are given permission. These double standard damages both sexes. Girls grow up ashamed of their sexuality, while boys grow up unaccountable for theirs.

It's time to replace shame with guidance. Teach both sons and daughters to respect themselves and others, to understand God's design, and to take responsibility for their choices.

4. "We don't talk about it."
Perhaps the most destructive mindset of all is the one that keeps everything hidden. The "don't ask, don't tell" culture has silenced victims, normalized abuse, and left generations emotionally crippled. Even as adults, many still hide behind that same veil, pretending indifference, denying desire, and carrying unspoken pain. Healing begins the moment we dare to speak.

Breaking the Generational Curse of Silence

For too long, families have equated silence with holiness. We thought that not talking about sex made us pure, when in fact, it made us ignorant. We must now become comfortable discussing uncomfortable things.

The next generation deserves truth, not taboos. They deserve to hear that sexuality, when guided by wisdom and faith, is not a curse but a blessing. The cycle of secrecy, shame, and misinformation must end with us.

Let's start teaching our children that their bodies are sacred, their choices matter, and their worth is not defined by anyone's judgment. Let's talk about consent, respect, and responsibility. Let's teach them that God's view of sex is not rooted in fear, but in love and purpose. Until we can do this openly, the demon we refuse to name will keep haunting our homes.

Healing generations of dysfunction begins with breaking the silence. We must be brave enough to speak where others were silent. Honest enough to teach where others hid. And compassionate enough to guide where others judged. Only then will we begin to reclaim one of God's greatest gifts from the grip of shame and secrecy.

Family Conversation Starters: Talking Through the Silence

Healthy conversations about sex and relationships don't begin with lectures—they begin with love. The goal is not to shame or shock, but to build understanding, mutual respect, and a safe space where truth replaces taboo.

Here are a few discussion prompts that can help families begin these much-needed conversations:

1. **What did you learn about sex growing up, and how did it shape your understanding of relationships?**
    - This question helps uncover generational beliefs and misunderstandings that need healing.

2. **Why do you think it's been so hard for families to talk openly about sex?**
    - It encourages self-awareness and compassion for the cultural roots of silence.

3. **How can we, as a family, create a safe space for honest discussions about sexuality, respect, and relationships?**
    - This shifts the focus from blame to building a healthy environment.

4. **What does God's design for intimacy teach us about love, respect, and commitment?**
    - This centers the conversation on faith and the spiritual purpose of sexuality.

5. **How can we respond with grace and support when someone in our family struggles or makes mistakes?**
    - This helps foster empathy instead of judgment, a key step in breaking cycles of shame.

Talking about sex will not corrupt our families; silence already has. Healing begins the moment truth enters the conversation. When families can speak about God's gift of intimacy without fear or condemnation, the generational curse of shame begins to break, and love takes its rightful place at the table.

Lessons from Chapter Twenty

1. A faulty understanding of sex and sexuality prolongs dysfunctional behaviours in families.
2. Demonizing sex allows perpetrators of sexual abuse to prey on the unsuspecting.
3. Though discussions about sex may be uncomfortable, there is a lot of benefit to having them.
4. When we lack accurate information about sex, our chances of receiving incorrect information increase significantly.
5. Breaking taboos surrounding sex will require honesty and courage. We must put aside faulty assumptions and seek useful information.
6. The veil of secrecy around sex is harmful, especially to those at risk of being abused by trusted family members.

Chapter Twenty-one

The dysfunction of superstition: When Fear Becomes Our Family Faith

Living Under the Shadow of Fear

Superstition has long been a silent member in many dysfunctional families. By superstition, I mean a belief not grounded in reason, fact, or knowledge, but in fear, folklore, and tradition. While most people hold some superstitious notions at one point or another, these beliefs become harmful when they begin to shape family behaviours, decisions, and identities.

In my family, superstition wasn't loud or theatrical, it was subtle, woven into daily speech, stories, and attitudes. I didn't recognize how deeply it had rooted itself until adulthood, when I began making decisions clouded by fear and suspicion. As a child, I never questioned it. I simply fell in line, accepting that this was "how things were."

Faith and Fear in the Same Breath

Dysfunctional families often blur the line between spirituality and superstition. I grew up watching this contradiction play out every day.

My grandmother was a devout woman of prayer. She read her Psalms faithfully, pleaded the blood of Jesus over our home, and prayed passionately for God's protection. But within those same prayers was a deep suspicion, someone in the community was *always* "trying to do her something."

It was common to hear churchgoers sing praises on Sunday, only to visit the *obeahman* on Monday. In our home, the Bible served both as a source of spiritual nourishment and a weapon against "duppy" attacks. For every problem, there was a Psalm to read, and a warning to watch out for who might be "working against you."

This blend of faith and fear created confusion. We called on Jesus, yet we feared shadows. We preached trust, yet we lived in constant suspicion.

When Superstition Explains Everything

I watched my family explain every hardship through superstition. If crops failed, if money ran low, if relationships fell apart, someone must have "turned us down."

As a boy, I accepted this without question. When I grew older, I began to see the cost of such thinking.

My grandfather, for example, suffered from what I now know was severe scoliosis. It left him with a pronounced hump in his back, for which he endured years of ridicule. Yet, rather than seeking medical help, the family insisted that someone had "worked obeah" on him because of jealousy over his small successes. He lived and died under that belie, an innocent victim of superstition and ignorance.

That's the danger of superstition: it replaces truth with myth and healing with helplessness. It offers comfort without solution.

The Fear of Kindness

Superstition bred distrust in my family. Every act of kindness was met with suspicion, every gift, every gesture, every friendly smile. We were warned not to eat or drink from anyone in the community because "dem might tun yuh dung."

While some of these cautions were born of wisdom in harsh times, many were simply chains of fear passed from one generation to another. As children, we learned to see danger in everything unfamiliar. I confess that I broke many of those rules—I ate at "forbidden" homes, drank from "tainted" cups, and I'm still here, alive, thriving, and walking in God's purpose.

That's when I began to understand *belief kills and belief cures.*

What we choose to believe shapes what we experience. If we constantly anticipate evil, we will see it everywhere. But if we focus on truth, goodness, and faith, we will find peace.

The Dark Side of Superstition

Superstition damages the emotional and psychological stability of families. It fuels fear instead of faith, avoidance instead of accountability.

It keeps people bound to the past, making decisions based not on wisdom, but on inherited fear. It breeds helplessness because it convinces us that unseen enemies, not our own choices, control our destiny.

Ignorance is not bliss, it is bondage. When superstition replaces knowledge, families are robbed of clarity, progress, and peace.

The Trap of Confirmation Bias

One of the most powerful forces keeping superstition alive is *confirmation bias,* our tendency to notice and remember only what confirms what we already believe.

If we believe that someone is trying to harm us, every misfortune will serve as proof. I saw this countless times growing up.

My grandmother once woke up to find white powder scattered at the front door. She immediately launched into spiritual warfare, pleading the blood of Jesus against evil workers. We later discovered it was flour my aunt had accidentally spilled the night before. But no amount of evidence could convince Grandma otherwise, she went to her grave believing the "enemy" had attacked.

That's the power of confirmation bias: it blinds us to truth and reinforces dysfunction. When superstition dictates our reality, facts lose their power.

Breaking Free from the Shackles of Superstition

Escaping the grip of superstition is not easy. It requires courage, education, and an open heart. For many, it feels safer to cling to old beliefs than to face the uncertainty of new truths. But growth only happens when we challenge what we've inherited.

To break free, we must begin by asking hard questions:

- Why do we believe what we believe?
- Where did those ideas come from?
- What evidence supports them, and what evidence contradicts them?

Freedom begins when one person in the family decides to think differently. Sometimes it takes only one voice of reason to start a revolution of healing.

The Role of Knowledge and Professional Help

The good news is that we are not doomed to repeat patterns of ignorance. In an age of access to reliable information, medical science, and counselling, we can finally separate superstition from spirituality.

Breaking free means replacing fear with understanding. It means seeking therapy, education, and prayer in their proper places. It means realizing that faith and logic are not enemies, they are allies when rightly applied.

For many, professional counselling provides the bridge between old thinking and new possibilities. It helps uncover how deeply superstition has shaped our fears and behaviours. It teaches us to discern truth from tradition, fact from folklore.

The Path to Freedom

Healing begins when we accept responsibility. Superstition thrives on blame; it convinces us that our struggles are someone else's fault. But the truth is this: **our choices, not curses, determine our direction.**

To truly heal our families, we must learn, unlearn, and relearn. We must admit that much of what we believed came from people who meant well but didn't know better. Once we shed the weight of those false beliefs, we can finally breathe, grow, and live freely.

There is no magic in freedom, just courage, truth, and the grace of God. Superstition is a poor substitute for spirituality. It demands fear where faith offers freedom. It keeps families bound when truth is ready to set them free. The time has come to let go of the "duppy stories" that keep us afraid of shadows. The only ghost we need to chase away is ignorance, and once that's gone, the light of truth will fill our homes again.

Reflection: Walking Away from Fear

1. What family beliefs or traditions have shaped your fears or decisions?
2. Are there "unquestioned truths" you've accepted that may be rooted in superstition rather than faith or fact?
3. How can you begin teaching the next generation to distinguish between spiritual discernment and irrational fear?
4. What role can education, counselling, and prayer play in freeing your family from superstition?

5. What would your life look like if you replaced fear with faith and knowledge?

Lessons from Chapter Twenty-one

1. Superstitious beliefs can inhibit the decision-making process needed to help overcome dysfunctional behaviours.
2. Misinterpretation of religious teachings gives room for the growth and continuation of dysfunctional behaviours.
3. Mixing religious and superstitious beliefs is dangerous for healthy families. It can lead us to make irrational decisions and faulty assumptions.
4. Superstition affects the emotional, psychological, and social well-being of the family unit.
5. Belief kills, and belief cures. Most of the time, it is the faulty beliefs we spend time indulging in that bring us harm.
6. Superstitions are a part of life, but they must not become our way of life.

Chapter Twenty-Two:

Gaslighting

When Truth is Twisted and the Mind Begins to Doubt

Coming to Terms with a Hidden Form of Abuse

Gaslighting is one of those words I didn't have in my vocabulary growing up, but I lived through it for years. When I began my master's degree in counselling and psychology, I encountered the term for the first time. Suddenly, the fog lifted. The pieces of a lifelong puzzle began to fit together.

I realized that I had not only been a victim of gaslighting, I had also, at times, unknowingly participated in it. This chapter is difficult to write because it forces me to confront both my wounds and my wrongs. But healing requires honesty, and this truth must be told.

Gaslighting is a form of emotional and psychological abuse that causes a person to question their perception of reality, their memories, and even their sanity. It is subtle but deadly, a slow erosion of trust in oneself. It can show up in marriages, friendships, workplaces, and especially in dysfunctional families.

The Faces of Gaslighting in Dysfunctional Families

In homes where dysfunction thrives, gaslighting often becomes the silent language of control. It's not always intentional; sometimes, it's simply learned behaviour passed from one wounded generation to the next. But its effects are devastating.

Here's how it often shows up:

1. **Invalidating Feelings**
   In many families, emotions are dismissed rather than embraced. When someone cries out in pain, they're told, *"You're too sensitive."* When they protest injustice, they hear, *"You're overreacting."* Over time, victims begin to doubt their feelings and suppress their truth.

2. **Distorting Reality**
   Gaslighters twist facts to maintain control. They rewrite history, deny promises made, and insist, *"That never happened."* This constant distortion leaves victims confused and unsure of their own memories.

3. **Playing the Victim**
   The gaslighter often turns the tables, portraying themselves as the wounded party. They use guilt as a weapon, manipulating others into apologizing for pain they didn't cause. In dysfunctional families, this dynamic keeps everyone trapped in cycles of blame and appeasement.

4. **Isolating the Victim**
   To maintain power, gaslighters divide and conquer. They sow mistrust among family members so that the victim has no allies. "Don't tell anyone; they won't believe you," becomes the unspoken rule.

5. Undermining Self-Esteem

Perhaps the cruelest effect of gaslighting is the erosion of self-worth. Victims begin to internalize the lies. They stop believing in their intelligence, goodness, or capacity to judge right from wrong. In homes where confidence was already fragile, gaslighting leaves people emotionally crippled.

The Toll on Family Life

Gaslighting poisons communication, fracturing trust and distorting love. In dysfunctional families, it can become so normalized that no one even sees it for what it is. Here are some of the major effects:

1. Communication Breakdown

Honest dialogue disappears. Family members become afraid to speak their minds, fearing ridicule or rejection. Emotional distance replaces connection.

2. Emotional Distress

Anxiety, depression, and chronic self-doubt take root. Victims of gaslighting often feel like they're "losing their mind." These emotional wounds don't heal easily—they linger long into adulthood.

3. Perpetuating Dysfunction

Gaslighting keeps the family focused on maintaining appearances instead of healing. The goal becomes peacekeeping, not truth-telling. The cycle of silence and suppression continues.

4. The Collapse of Trust

Without trust, love cannot thrive. Gaslighting destroys the foundation of trust, leaving every relationship fragile and fearful.

5. Long-Term Consequences

Adults who grew up in gaslighting environments struggle to trust others, or themselves. They second-guess their memories, doubt their instincts, and often find themselves in new relationships that mirror their painful pasts.

Breaking the Cycle: The Road to Recovery

Escaping the grip of gaslighting is not easy. It takes courage to reclaim your truth after years of manipulation. Healing begins the moment you recognize what's happening and choose to step into the light of awareness.

Here's how recovery unfolds:

1. Recognize the Manipulation

The first step is awareness. Gaslighting thrives in confusion; clarity destroys its power. Seeing the pattern for what it is allows you to stop taking the blame for someone else's deception. Therapy can help connect the dots and name the behaviours for what they are, abuse.

2. Rebuild Self-Esteem

Gaslighting leaves deep wounds of self-doubt. Healing means relearning how to trust your perceptions and feelings. Counselling helps rebuild that inner confidence and reminds you of your inherent worth and strength.

3. Develop Healthy Coping Strategies

Victims of gaslighting often live in constant anxiety. Learning coping skills such as emotional regulation, mindfulness, and assertiveness helps reclaim control. You learn to respond rather than react, and to stand firm in your truth.

4. Establish Boundaries

In dysfunctional homes, boundaries are often blurred or nonexistent. Recovery requires learning to say no without guilt. Healthy boundaries protect your peace and give you the emotional space to heal.

5. Seek Validation and Support

One of the cruelest effects of gaslighting is isolation. Reconnecting with safe, supportive people; trusted friends, therapists, mentors, or faith leaders, helps you rebuild a network of truth-tellers who affirm your reality.

6. Move Toward Independence

Freedom from gaslighting sometimes requires physical and emotional distance. That may mean creating independence through education, work, or a new living environment. Each step toward autonomy strengthens your ability to make decisions from a place of truth rather than fear.

The Light at the End of the Tunnel

Healing from gaslighting is a journey of rediscovering yourself. It's about learning to trust your inner voice again, the one that was silent for so long. You learn that your feelings are valid, your memories are real, and your truth matters.

Counselling and faith work hand in hand here: therapy helps you rebuild your psychological foundation, while faith reminds you that your worth was never lost, only hidden under the rubble of deception.

The journey is not easy, but every step forward reclaims another piece of your freedom. You learn that your identity was never defined by the gaslighter's lies but by the truth of who God says you are

Gaslighting is one of the most subtle but devastating forms of emotional abuse. It makes you doubt your truth until you forget who you are.

But here's the miracle: the moment you begin to believe in your own voice again, the spell is broken. The lies lose their grip, the fog begins to lift, and truth, God's truth, becomes your anchor once more.

You were never crazy. You were conditioned to doubt your clarity. Now, it's time to reclaim it.

Reflection: Reclaiming Your Reality

1. Have you ever questioned your own memory or emotions because someone repeatedly told you that you were wrong?
2. How has gaslighting, whether intentional or not, shaped your sense of self?
3. What boundaries do you need to establish to protect your mental and emotional peace?
4. Who in your life can you trust to affirm your truth without judgment or manipulation?
5. What step can you take today to begin healing from the effects of gaslighting?

Conclusion

Stepping Into a New Legacy

Shattering the glasshouse is not merely a concept, it is a call to courage, healing, and transformation. Throughout this book, we have peeled back some of the layers of dysfunction that shape families across generations. We have examined the hidden wounds, the unspoken truths, the cultural norms, and the inherited behaviours that have shaped our lives. And we have seen, again and again, that dysfunction thrives in darkness, but healing thrives in light.

Every chapter has been a step toward uncovering the truth that many of us have lived but were never taught to name. The truth that what we call "generational curses" are often generational patterns, behaviours repeated because no one knew another way. Pain passed down because no one paused to heal. Silence preserved because no one dared to speak.

But now you know.
And knowing gives you power.
Power to choose.
Power to change.
Power to build a new legacy.
A New Way Forward

If this book has done its work, then something inside you has awakened. Perhaps a memory resurfaced, a pattern became clear, or a question you've never dared to ask has finally taken shape. This is not by accident. Awareness is the doorway to transformation.

But awareness alone is not enough. Change requires intention. Healing requires action and renewal requires courage. You cannot undo the actions of the generations before you, but you can stop them from shaping the generations after you. The future of your family does not have to resemble its past. You can be the interruption. You can be the difference. You can be the first voice in your lineage to say: ***"It ends with me."***

From Survival to Wholeness

Many of us were raised in households where love was present but poorly expressed. Where discipline was given, but communication was withheld. Where secrets were protected, but hearts were left unguarded. Where loyalty was demanded, but emotional safety was missing. These experiences created adults who are still learning how to love, how to trust, how to feel worthy, and how to speak life.

If this is you, hear this clearly:

> ***You are not broken beyond repair.***
> ***You are not defined by where you came from.***
> ***You are not destined to repeat what you endured.***

Healing may not erase the past, but it transforms the way the past lives within you. Your journey from dysfunction to healing is sacred. It requires gentleness, honesty, and compassion toward yourself. It may involve difficult conversations, new boundaries, or seeking professional help, choices that your parents or grandparents never had the freedom or knowledge to pursue.

Healing yourself is not betrayal; it is honour. It honours the generations before you by becoming what they never had the chance to be. It honours your children by giving them what you never received.

The Role of Faith in Healing

As Caribbean people, faith has always been part of our DNA. But faith without transformation becomes routine. And healing without faith becomes incomplete. The God who formed you did not design your family to live in cycles of chaos, silence, fear, or brokenness. His vision for family has always been love, connection, mutual support, and growth.

You may have walked through trauma, but trauma does not have the final say. God does. You may have been wounded by the people meant to protect you, but healing is still possible. You may have lived in patterns of dysfunction, but grace can break every chain that behaviour cannot.

Your story, like Joseph's, may include betrayal, hurt, abandonment, or rejection. But also, like Joseph, God can use every chapter for good. Even the painful ones. Even the ones you don't talk about. Even the ones you wish you could forget. Grace does not erase history, it rewrites destiny.

A Legacy Reimagined

If you take nothing else from this book, take this: **You have the power to create a healthier story for your family.** Every choice you make, how you speak, how you discipline, how you love, how you heal, how you seek help, shapes the legacy you leave. Your children and grandchildren will one day look back on this moment and recognize it as the point where everything changed.

You may not see the full results immediately. Healing is both a process and a journey. But the small steps matter:

- ✓ *Choosing not to repeat an unhealthy behavior*
- ✓ *Speaking a kind word where harshness once lived*
- ✓ *Listening before reacting*
- ✓ *Setting boundaries you were never taught to have*
- ✓ *Seeking help without shame*
- ✓ *Asking honest questions*
- ✓ *Confronting silence with truth*
- ✓ *Replacing fear with faith*
- ✓ *Practicing love with intention*

These simple acts, repeated consistently, have the power to change an entire lineage.

A Final Word

I wrote this book not as an expert looking down from a place of perfection, but as a fellow traveller, one who has lived the pain of dysfunction, but also the joy of healing. I am still on the journey, still learning, still growing, and still choosing daily to build a healthier legacy for my family.

I pray that this book becomes a tool for your transformation, a lantern guiding you from the dim corridors of past hurts into the wide, open spaces of emotional freedom. I pray it challenges the way you see your family, but even more, the way you see yourself. And I pray that as you move forward, you will walk with courage, compassion, and conviction.

- ✓ *May you be the one who shatters the glasshouse.*
- ✓ *May you be the one who breaks the silence.*
- ✓ *May you be the one who interrupts the cycle.*
- ✓ *May you be the one who chooses healing over hurt.*
- ✓ *May you be the one who builds a home, not a prison.*
- ✓ *May you be the one who leaves a legacy of love, not fear.*
- ✓ *May you be the one who turns pain into purpose.*

The glasshouse has cracked. Now it is time to build something new. And you are the builder.

References

Economy, Peter (2015) 26 Brilliant Quotes on the Super Power of Words, Retrieved J

June 8, 2022 https://www.inc.com/peter-economy/26-brilliant-quotes-on-the-super-power-of-words.html

Gerlach, Peter, K (2015) Break the Cycle: Avoid Family Secrets Guard Your Kids Against Shame and Fear Retrieved June 11, 2022 http://sfhelp.org/fam/secrets.htm

James, Kizanne (2020) We Need to Talk About Everyday Colorism in the Caribbean. Retrieved June 13, 2020 https://www.girlsglobe.org/2020/09/09/we-need-to-talk-about-everyday-colorism-in-the-caribbean/?doing_wp_cron=1655149266.4679319858551025390625

Li, Pamela (2022) What Is A Dysfunctional Family & How To Break The Cycle, Retrieved July 29, 2022 https://www.parentingforbrain.com/dysfunctional-family/

Trivia Faith Blog (2023) The Power Of Forgiveness – 10 Important Thinks You Need To

Know Retrieved January 24, 2022 https://triviafaithblog.com/the-power-of- forgiveness/

William, Jackson, D (2013) Are Jamaicans really that stigmatizing? A comparison of mental health help-seeking attitudes, Retrieved July 31, 2022, https://pubmed.ncbi.nlm.nih.gov/24756657/

Zink, David (2008) Family Systems Theory: Secrets, Circular Causality and Assessments Procedure, Retrieved June 12, 2022 https://media.thegospelcoalition.org/wp-content/uploads/2017/11/10225533/MFC-L10-transcription-edited.pdf

Glossary

Caribbean Colloquial Terms

"Ah jus suh mi stay" / "Ah suh mi stay" – A Jamaican expression meaning *"that's just how I am."* Often used to excuse or justify negative behaviors instead of working to change them.

"Bad luck a falla wi" – A common Caribbean saying suggesting that misfortune is following the family, as though they are doomed to bad outcomes no matter what.

"Black sheep" – A term used in many cultures (including Jamaica) to describe someone seen as different, rebellious, or a disgrace to the family. Being labeled this way often causes deep hurt and rejection.

"Crasses a falla wi" – A phrase suggesting that a curse or misfortune is hanging over the family.

"Dem have bad blood" / "It inna dem blood" – Expressions meaning that negative traits or destructive behaviors are part of a family's nature and are inherited from one generation to the next.

"Nutten too black, nuh good" – A saying that reflects colorism within families and communities, where darker skin is looked down upon and lighter skin is seen as more desirable.

Obeah man – In Caribbean culture, a folk spiritualist or healer that people often visit for help with problems, protection, or revenge, outside of Christian practices.

Reader woman – Similar to an obeah man, but usually female. A woman believed to have spiritual powers to "read" people's situations and offer solutions, often through rituals or divination.

Tit-for-tat mentality – A way of describing the habit of responding to hurt with more hurt. In Caribbean families, this often shows up as harsh words or actions passed back and forth, keeping dysfunction alive.

High complexion – A local term used to describe someone with a lighter skin tone, often linked to social privilege or beauty standards.

Yard – A colloquial Caribbean term for a shared living space or home, often where multiple families or extended relatives live together.

Cinderella, the uninvited stepsister – A figurative expression describing how some family members feel excluded, unvalued, or treated as lesser during gatherings.

Psychological & Family Terms

Dysfunctional family – A family where unhealthy patterns (like abuse, neglect, poor communication, or favoritism) are repeated, often leading to emotional harm for its members.

Generational cycle – The idea that behaviors, habits, and struggles (such as abuse, poverty, or addiction) are passed down from one generation to the next unless someone makes a conscious effort to break the pattern.

Generational curse – A belief (common in some cultures and religious circles) that negative events or behaviors in a family are caused by curses passed down spiritually. In psychology, these patterns are better understood as learned behaviors, trauma, and family dynamics.

Family secrets – Hidden truths or events in a family (such as infidelity, abuse, or financial troubles) that members choose not to talk about. While meant to "protect" the family, they often cause confusion, mistrust, and long-term harm.

Colorism – Prejudice or discrimination within the same racial or ethnic group, based on skin tone. For example, preferring lighter skin over darker skin.

Verbal abuse – The use of words to insult, belittle, or control another person. In families, this can have long-term psychological effects, especially on children.

Trauma – Deep emotional or psychological wounds caused by distressing experiences, such as abuse, neglect, or violence. Unhealed trauma often shapes family dysfunction across generations.

Conflict resolution skills – The ability to resolve disagreements constructively and peacefully rather than through quarrels, violence, or avoidance.

Identity crisis – A period of uncertainty or confusion about one's sense of self, often triggered by negative experiences or inconsistent affirmations.

Low self-esteem – A negative view of one's worth or abilities, often rooted in repeated criticism, comparison, or rejection.

Generational trauma – The passing down of unhealthy behaviours, beliefs, or emotional pain from one generation to another.

Biblical & Spiritual Concepts

Abundant life – A biblical principle (John 10:10) referring to the fullness of life in Christ, including peace, joy, and purpose beyond material success.

Life and death in the tongue – From Proverbs 18:21, the teaching that our words have the power to either harm or heal. The words we speak can affect our own lives and the lives of others profoundly.

Power of words – A biblical principle emphasizing that speech reflects the heart and has the potential to bless or curse (see James 3:1–12, Matthew 12:34).

Forgiveness – Letting go of resentment or the desire for revenge, as taught in multiple passages including Ephesians 4:32. Forgiveness is essential for breaking cycles of dysfunction and healing relationships.

Tongue (biblical metaphor) – Represents human speech; Scripture repeatedly highlights that it can be difficult to control and has the power to build up or destroy.

Grace in speech – From Colossians 4:6, the principle of speaking with kindness, respect, and wisdom, ensuring our words uplift rather than harm.

Prodigal child – From the parable of the *Prodigal Son* (Luke 15:11–32); refers to a child who squanders opportunities or brings disappointment but later returns seeking restoration.

Glasshouse (shattering the glasshouse) – A metaphor for breaking patterns of secrecy, hypocrisy, and pretense in families, so truth and healing can emerge.

Healing and restoration – Biblical themes emphasizing God's desire to mend brokenness, reconcile relationships, and bring wholeness to individuals and families.

Self-Assessment Tool

Where Am I on My Healing Journey?

A personal guide to breaking cycles and building a healthier legacy.

SECTION 1 — IDENTIFYING FAMILY PATTERNS

A. Family Environment Checklist

For each statement, circle: **Yes / No / Not Sure**

1. My family avoids discussing painful or uncomfortable topics.
   Yes / No / Not Sure

2. I grew up in a home where negative or harsh words were more common than affirming ones.
   Yes / No / Not Sure

3. Family conflict was often handled through shouting, silence, or avoidance.
   Yes / No / Not Sure

4. Corporal punishment ("licks," "beatings," etc.) was the main form of discipline.
   Yes / No / Not Sure

5. Boundaries were unclear or not respected.
   Yes / No / Not Sure

6. Secrets were common and rarely challenged.
   Yes / No / Not Sure

7. Superstitious beliefs influenced my family's decisions or behaviour.
   Yes / No / Not Sure

8. Family members played roles (e.g., "the troublemaker," "the black sheep," "the quiet one").
   Yes / No / Not Sure

9. Emotional expression was discouraged or seen as weakness.
   Yes / No / Not Sure

10. My family taught me to "keep problems in-house" instead of seeking help.
    Yes / No / Not Sure

Reflection:
Which of these patterns still affect you today?

SECTION 2 — PERSONAL BELIEFS & BEHAVIOURS

B. What Did You Inherit?

Rate each item:

1 — Not at all

2 — Sometimes

3 — Often

4 — Very often

How often do you:

1. Speak harshly when frustrated?
2. Struggle to express emotions honestly?
3. Fear rejection or criticism?
4. Avoid conflict even when necessary?
5. Assume negative labels about yourself (e.g., "not good enough," "too much")?
6. Keep secrets to "protect the family"?
7. Expect the worst because "that's how my family is"?
8. Feel responsible for fixing everyone else's problems?
9. Feel guilty setting boundaries?
10. Repeat behaviours you disliked growing up?

Reflection:
Which of these habits do you want to change?

SECTION 3 —
EMOTIONAL WELL-BEING CHECK-IN

C. Your Current Emotional Landscape

Circle the number that best describes your experience:

How often do you feel…

1. Overwhelmed or exhausted emotionally?

   1 — 2 — 3 — 4

2. Anger that you struggle to express or manage?

   1 — 2 — 3 — 4

3. Fear of becoming like your parents or caregivers?

   1 — 2 — 3 — 4

4. Shame about your family background?

   1 — 2 — 3 — 4

5. Anxiety around family gatherings?

   1 — 2 — 3 — 4

6. Confusion about your own identity or worth?

   1 — 2 — 3 — 4

7. Emotional distance from family members?

   1 — 2 — 3 — 4

8. Pressure to keep the peace even when hurting?

   1 — 2 — 3 — 4

9. Loneliness despite being around others?

   1 — 2 — 3 — 4

10. Desire for a healthier, more peaceful life?

    1 — 2 — 3 — 4

Reflection:

What do these emotions reveal about your healing needs?

SECTION 4 — COMMUNICATION PATTERNS

D. How Do You Speak? How Do You Listen?

Check all that apply to you:

When communicating, I often:

- ☐ React before thinking.
- ☐ Raise my voice to be heard.
- ☐ Shut down instead of speaking up.
- ☐ Speak harshly without intending to hurt.
- ☐ Avoid deep conversations.
- ☐ Apologize even when I've done nothing wrong.
- ☐ Struggle to forgive myself or others.
- ☐ Feel unheard or misunderstood.
- ☐ Believe silence keeps the peace.
- ☐ Use encouraging words intentionally.

Reflection:

Which habits do you want to strengthen or release?

SECTION 5 — BOUNDARIES & RELATIONSHIPS

E. Boundary Check

Answer True or False:

1. I struggle to say "no" without feeling guilty.
2. I often allow people to disrespect my emotional space.
3. I feel obligated to help others even when I am overwhelmed.
4. I confuse setting boundaries with being unkind.
5. I sometimes return to relationships that hurt me.
6. I caretake others at the expense of myself.
7. I believe it is my duty to keep the family together.
8. I fear family members' reactions to my choices.
9. I often put myself last.
10. I want healthier boundaries but don't know where to begin.

Reflection:

Where do you need stronger boundaries?

SECTION 6 — HEALING & HOPE

F. Your Readiness for Change

Rate your level of readiness:

1 — Not ready

2 — Maybe

3 — Ready

4 — Fully committed

1. I am ready to break generational patterns.
2. I am ready to speak honestly about my experiences.
3. I am ready to learn healthier communication tools.
4. I am ready to seek counselling or professional help.
5. I am ready to parent differently from how I was raised.
6. I am ready to set boundaries—even if others dislike it.
7. I am ready to forgive myself for what I didn't know.
8. I am ready to pursue emotional well-being.
9. I am ready to build a healthy family legacy.
10. I am ready to shatter the glasshouse.

SECTION 7 — YOUR HEALING PLAN

G. Three Big Changes I Want to Make

1. ______________________________
2. ______________________________
3. ______________________________

H. Three Generational Patterns I Refuse to Repeat

1. ______________________________

2. ______________________________

3. ______________________________

I. Three Practices I Will Begin This Month

1. ______________________________

2. ______________________________

3. ______________________________

SECTION 8 — AFFIRMATIONS FOR YOUR JOURNEY

Choose the ones that resonate—or write your own:

- I am worthy of healing.
- My past does not define my future.
- I can learn new patterns and unlearn old ones.
- I am not responsible for my family's dysfunction, but I can change mine.
- My voice is valuable. My story matters.
- I break cycles with courage, not perfection.
- I am building a legacy of love, truth, and strength.

10-Point Family Healing Roadmap

A step-by-step guide for breaking dysfunctional cycles and building a healthier legacy

1. Acknowledge the Reality of Dysfunction
Healing begins with honesty.

Families cannot change what they refuse to acknowledge.

Recognizing the patterns—anger, secrecy, poor communication, abuse, neglect, confusion, fear—is the first breakthrough.

Key Questions:

- What behaviours in my family have caused long-term harm?
- What patterns do I see repeating across generations?

2. Challenge the "That's Just How We Stay" Mindset
This belief is one of the strongest barriers to transformation. Caribbean families often normalize dysfunction because it feels familiar—but familiarity is not health.

New Declaration:
"I can do differently because I know differently."

3. Learn the Art of Healthy Communication
Words are powerful enough to build or destroy.

Healing families replace shouting, silence, and sarcasm with conversations rooted in truth, respect, and empathy.

Immediate Practice:
Pause → Think → Speak with intention.

4. Break the Culture of Secrets
Hidden pain breeds more pain.

Families heal when secrecy is replaced with truth, accountability, and compassion.

Ask:

- What secrets are we keeping?
- Who is being harmed by this silence?

5. Address Generational Trauma Consciously
Trauma does not vanish with time. it mutates.

Understanding how past wounds shaped present behaviours helps families move from judgment to healing.

Tools:

- Journaling
- Family conversations
- Therapy sessions
- Spiritual reflection

6. Redefine Discipline Through Love, Not Fear
Harsh corporal punishment passed down as "tradition" often produces fear, rebellion, and emotional shut-down.

Healthy discipline teaches, guides, and protects, it does not terrorize.

Healthy Discipline Includes:

- Clear boundaries
- Calm explanations
- Age-appropriate consequences
- Emotional safety

7. Set Boundaries Without Guilt

Healing requires space, protection, and emotional clarity.

Boundaries are expressions of love, for yourself and for others, not rejection.

Examples:

- "I choose not to discuss this when we're angry."
- "I will not tolerate disrespect."
- "I need time to process before responding."

8. Seek Professional & Spiritual Support

Counselling, therapy, and pastoral care are NOT signs of weakness; they are acts of courage.

Breaking generational cycles often requires tools and insights we were never taught at home.

Remember:

We pray AND we pursue help.

Faith and therapy walk hand in hand.

9. Rewrite the Family Narrative

Every family has stories of pain, but also stories of resilience.

Healing means reclaiming your voice, redefining your identity, and choosing the legacy you want to pass on.

Exercise:

Write a new family declaration beginning with:

"In this generation, we choose..."

10. Commit to the Long Journey of Change

Change is not instant. It is not linear.

There will be setbacks, but transformation requires consistency, humility, and hope.

Final Encouragement:
Every small step you take, every truth spoken, every boundary set, every harmful pattern broken, shatters the glasshouse a little more. Future generations will thank you for the courage you showed today.

Next Steps: Your Action Guide to Breaking the Cycle

Healing family dysfunction is not a one-time decision, it is a sustained journey.

This guide provides clear, simple steps readers can begin immediately as they work toward transformation.

1. Reflect on What You've Learned

Before rushing into action, take time to process the insights gained from the book.

Action Steps:

- Identify the chapter that impacted you the most and journal why.
- List 3 dysfunctional patterns you recognize in your own family or upbringing.
- Identify which of these patterns you are still carrying today.

2. Choose One Area to Work on First

Trying to fix everything at once leads to overwhelm.

Healing begins with a single focused step.

Action Steps:

- Circle ONE behaviour or mindset you want to change (e.g., communication style, secrecy, anger, boundary-setting).
- Write one sentence declaring your intention to break that pattern.

3. Start a Personal Healing Plan

Your healing must begin with you before it can affect your family.

Action Steps:

- Create a weekly "emotional check-in" time to assess your stress, triggers, and emotional needs.
- Practice a grounding activity daily (prayer, meditation, journaling, deep breathing).
- Record small wins, these will motivate you on difficult days.

4. Open One Honest Conversation

Breaking the glasshouse requires communication, not confrontation.

Action Steps:

- Identify one safe person you can begin talking to (sibling, spouse, cousin, trusted friend).
- Share one truth you've been afraid to discuss.
- Agree on one small change you can make together.

5. Break One Silence

Choose one secret, pattern, or issue that has been covered for generations, and name it.

Action Steps:

- Write the secret or unspoken issue in your journal.

- Acknowledge how it has affected your life.
- Decide whether it needs to be shared with someone else or addressed privately through therapy or spiritual support.

6. Create Healthier Communication Habits
Words can either reinforce dysfunction or open the door to healing.

Action Steps:

- Practice "Pause → Breathe → Respond" daily.
- Replace one negative phrase you use often with a healthier alternative.
- Incorporate one affirmation into your family's daily routine.

7. Develop Emotional and Physical Boundaries
Boundaries are not rejection, they are protection.

Action Steps:

- Identify one behaviour you will no longer tolerate (shouting, guilt-tripping, name-calling).
- Write the boundary clearly and practice saying it aloud.
- Enforce the boundary calmly and consistently for 30 days.

8. Seek Professional or Spiritual Guidance
Healing is not meant to happen alone.

Action Steps:

- Decide whether you need counselling, mentorship, pastoral support, or group therapy.
- Research at least two professionals or safe spaces to explore.

- Commit to one consultation, even if it's just an introductory session.

9. Build a Support Circle
Transformation is easier with partners, not isolation.

Action Steps:

- Identify 2–3 people in your life who bring peace, support, and wisdom.
- Establish a monthly check-in with them.
- Decide together how you can hold each other accountable for growth.

10. Create Your Family's New Legacy Statement
A new legacy must be intentional, not accidental.

Action Steps:

- Write a family declaration that begins with:

  "In this generation, we choose…"

- Share it with your children, siblings, or spouse.
- Put it somewhere visible (fridge, journal, family WhatsApp group).

Final Encouragement
Transformation does not require perfection; it requires commitment. Every step you take weakens the power of generational dysfunction and strengthens the foundation for the generation after you.

You are not merely breaking cycles; you are building a future.

✦

A Reflective Prayer

(For Healing, Renewal, and Breaking Generational Cycles)

Heavenly Father,
I come before You with a heart open to truth, healing, and transformation.
You know the wounds I carry—those I acknowledge and those buried deep within me.
You know the stories written across generations, the pain hidden behind silence, and the struggles wrapped in secrecy.
Today, Lord, I surrender them all to You.

Father, I thank You that I am not bound by the dysfunction of yesterday.
I thank You that generational cycles do not define my destiny.
I thank You that what was broken can be healed, what was hidden can be brought to light,
and what was meant for harm can be used for good.

Lord, give me the courage to confront the things I once feared,
the strength to make different choices,
and the wisdom to walk in new patterns of peace and purpose.
Teach me to speak life-giving words,
to love with compassion,

and to build my family with grace, not fear.

Where there has been anger, bring calm.
Where there has been silence, bring truth.
Where there has been shame, bring freedom.
Where there has been division, bring reconciliation.
Where there has been trauma, bring deep and lasting healing.

Father, break every cycle that does not honor You—
cycles of hurt, secrecy, mistrust, violence, and emotional neglect.
Rewrite the story of my family, beginning with me.
Let Your light fill every room of our hearts,
and let the generations after me inherit blessing instead of brokenness.

Lord, help me forgive those who were themselves wounded and could not give what they never received.
Help me release resentment and walk forward without the weight of the past.
Help me extend grace while establishing healthy boundaries that protect my peace.

I ask that You surround my home with Your presence.
Let love dwell here.
Let healing dwell here.
Let Your Spirit dwell here.

And as I continue this journey, remind me that I am not alone.
You walk with me.
You strengthen me.
You restore me.
You transform me.

Thank You, Lord, for the new beginning You have given me.

Thank You for the hope that rises beyond the glasshouse of yesterday.
Thank You for the purpose that awaits me and the abundant life You have promised.

May my life and my family become living testimonies of Your healing power.
May Your will be done in us and through us, from this generation to the next.

In the mighty name of Jesus Christ,
Amen.

About the Author

Paul A. Blake, M.A.

- ***Engaging***
- ***Empowering***
- ***Energetic***

Paul A. Blake is a dynamic author, certified coach and mentor, leadership trainer, minister of religion, and motivational speaker whose voice continues to impact audiences across the Caribbean, North America, and beyond. With an energizing presence and a message rooted in faith, purpose, and personal transformation, Paul is on a mission to help people live abundant lives filled with clarity, confidence, and conviction.

A passionate communicator, Paul has inspired thousands through seminars, workshops, corporate trainings, keynote presentations, and media appearances. His influence extends across Jamaica and the wider Caribbean, including Cayman, Grenada, Barbados, Aruba, Cuba, and the United States, where he has delivered high-impact presentations on leadership, personal development, marriage enrichment, and purposeful living. He is also the co-host of *Level Up Your Marriage*, a relationship-building podcast he presents alongside his wife, Racquel Blake.

Paul holds a Master of Arts in Pastoral Psychology and Counselling from the International University of the Caribbean, a Bachelor of Arts in Theology from the University of the West Indies, a Bachelor of Science in Religious Studies from the Jamaica School of Preaching and Biblical Studies. As a writer, he is the author of several acclaimed books, including *It's Not Rocket Science: Simplifying the Complexities of Marriage*, co-authored with Racquel. His first book, *Words to Inspire Volume One*, was nominated for the Indie Legacy Book Cover Design of the Year.

Growing up in poverty and overcoming early struggles with self-worth, Paul carries a powerful personal story of resilience and faith. Today, he channels those experiences into helping people break free from limitations, discover their God-given purpose, and pursue abundant living. His mantra, *"I can do all things through Christ,"* guides both his life and his leadership.

Paul is the CEO and founder of Words Worthit Motivational Speaking & Training Co. Ltd. and Words Worthit Publishers, organizations dedicated to transforming lives through the power of words, coaching, and personal development.

A highly sought-after speaker, Paul, delivers keynote addresses and trainings on:

- Coaching and Mentoring
- Personal Development & Purpose-Driven Living
- Marriage and Family Counselling
- Parenting & Fatherhood
- Leadership Through Change and Uncertainty
- Men's Empowerment and Spiritual Growth

Paul A. Blake believes that abundant living is purposeful living. With each message, he empowers individuals and teams to rise above fear, embrace their potential, and step boldly into the life they were created to live.

www.ingramcontent.com/pod-product-compliance
Lightning Source LLC
La Vergne TN
LVHW020510100826
845148LV00003B/738

* 9 7 8 9 7 6 9 7 1 2 0 6 5 *